A NEW GRAMMAR COMPANION
FOR TEACHERS

BEVERLY DEREWIANKA

PETAA
PRIMARY ENGLISH TEACHING
ASSOCIATION AUSTRALIA

First published April 2011
Reprinted 2012, 2013, 2015, 2018, 2019
Copyright © Primary English Teaching Association, PETAA and Beverly Derewianka
ISBN 978 1 875622 90 0

National Library of Australia Cataloguing-in-Publication entry

Derewianka, Beverly, 1946-

A new grammar companion for teachers/Beverly Derewianka.
2nd ed.
ISBN: 9781875622900

English language – Grammar – Study and teaching (Primary)
Grammar, Comparative and general – Study and teaching (Primary)

Other Authors/Contributors: Primary English Teaching Association (Australia)

Dewey Number: 415

Copying for Educational Purposes

Copying for other purposes

Edited by Rema Gnanadickam, Zodiac Publishing Services
Index by Fiona Sim
Cover, text design and illustrations by Pamela Horsnell, Juno Creative Services
Typeset by Jacqui Fry, Craftype
Printed at Ligare Pty Ltd
138 Bonds Road Riverwood NSW 2210

The paper this book is printed on is in accordance with the rules of the Forest Stewardship Council®. The FSC® promotes environmentally responsible, socially beneficial and economically viable management of the world's forests.

PREFACE

Over the past few years, e:lit has published a number of books dealing directly or indirectly with questions of grammar. In the widely read *Exploring How Texts Work* (1990) by Beverly Derewianka certain grammatical features were highlighted in terms of how they operated within particular genres. This provided insights into how grammar could be treated functionally in context. John Collerson followed this up with a more detailed account of English grammar from a functional perspective in *English Grammar: A Functional Approach* (1994). This work was groundbreaking, introducing teachers to a different way of looking at language based on Halliday's *Functional Grammar*. In 1997, PETA published John Collerson's *Grammar in Teaching* which demonstrated a rich variety of ways in which functional grammar could be drawn upon in classroom activities.

So why do we need another book on grammar? The increasing interest in grammar throughout Australia and its appearance in a number of syllabus and curriculum documents — including the *Australian Curriculum: English* — has stimulated a demand for a handbook which familiarises teachers with the basics of the English grammatical system. While teachers have been excited by the potential of working with a functional approach to grammar, many are still a bit daunted by its newness and the terminology. This book is intended therefore as a bridge for teachers between what they already know about grammar and how they might extend that knowledge to include a more functional perspective.

A New Grammar Companion employs standard grammatical terminology which is familiar to teachers and the community, but it also uses terms which allow for a more functional interpretation.

This book is not intended as a comprehensive grammar of English. It provides an overview of those features of grammar that have been found to be useful in school contexts in terms of supporting and extending students' ability to use English productively for educational purposes. For further detail on any of the aspects, you are encouraged to consult more detailed descriptions of English (as in some of the references in the final chapter).

Unlike the previous edition, which was organised according to grammatical categories, this edition is organised around the main functions that language plays in our lives: expressing and connecting ideas, interacting with others and creating coherent texts. Another major difference is that the content now extends into secondary schooling, dealing with the language challenges faced by older students.

We are sure that *A New Grammar Companion* will become a well-thumbed reference and guide, which will truly keep you company and provide reassurance as you introduce students to the fascinating workings of grammar.

PETAA
Primary English Teaching Association Australia

1 Introduction

What is grammar?

While there are many technical definitions of grammar, for our purposes we could simply say that grammar is a way of describing how a language works to make meaning.

Why learn about grammar?

We learn about grammar to:

- be able to reflect on how the English language works
- be able to use language effectively, appropriately and accurately
- understand how different kinds of meaning are created through the use of different grammatical forms so that we can control and shape those meanings more skilfully and effectively ourselves
- critically analyse texts so we can understand how grammar has been used to achieve certain effects
- examine patterns of language and word choices so that we can appreciate, interpret and create well-constructed texts
- have a shared language for teaching and learning about the main features of the English language.

A multi-purpose grammar

The description of grammar provided here has been designed so that teachers can use it for a number of different purposes: for exploring how language functions to create different types of meaning; for understanding the structure or formation of various language features; and for anticipating where students might need particular assistance with certain features. The book therefore includes sections on looking at meaning, looking at form, and troubleshooting.

If you are primarily interested in **meaning**, you might like to focus on those sections that discuss how our linguistic choices create certain meanings. In this book we are viewing grammar as a resource – an array of possibilities from which we can choose. Learning grammar in this sense is seen as extending a learner's potential to make and interpret meanings.

If you are primarily interested in **form**, you might like to focus on those sections that explain how various grammatical features are structured. A traditional motive for teaching about grammar has been the development of an analytical approach to language – an ability to 'reason grammatically' – along with the identification and naming of different grammatical categories, providing students with a language for talking about language. Knowing how language is structured helps us to deal with questions such as:

- What does a noun group consist of?
- How are different verb tenses formed?
- What does a clause look like?
- How are messages combined to form sentences?

Preferably, however, the focus will be on the relationship between **meaning** and **form**. In this book, we look at how the different grammatical categories are involved in the construction of meaning with questions such as:

- What range of meanings do verbs express?
- How can my choice of nouns affect the meaning of the text?
- How can I use certain types of adjectives to express my opinion about something?
- Which grammatical features are involved in skills such as classifying, defining, describing, generalising, exemplifying?
- Which linguistic features can help me produce a text that is coherent and cohesive?
- How do grammatical patterns change from text to text? Why and with what effect?
- How does the context affect the kinds of grammatical choices made?

If you are concerned about the kinds of problems students might encounter, look for the **Troubleshooting** notes. There are certain linguistic structures that often cause problems, particularly for young students and EAL/ESL[1] learners. In many cases, the problems will sort themselves out over time. Often, however, it is useful for the teacher to be able to identify trouble spots so that the problem can be explained or so that activities can be designed to address the difficulty. ESL learners will need a much greater focus on developing their control over English grammatical structures and meaning.

It is this area that many people associate with the learning of grammar: the correction of 'mistakes'. This is a legitimate area of concern. Students' language is often judged by their control over certain linguistic features, and this can be a significant factor in examinations, job applications, and so on. It is important, however, not to let this get out of perspective. Many 'problems' reflect students' use of social dialects, especially in the spoken mode: *he done it*; *me and him are going home*. In the written mode, however, there are probably only a dozen or so problem structures that regularly crop up – and most of them are to do with punctuation, not grammar. Typical of these are issues such as the use of 'comma splices' (*It was getting late, we went home.*); 'run on sentences' (*The cows got out of the paddock they ran through the streets the farmer couldn't catch them.*); and 'sentence fragments' (*There were lots of animals. Such as kangaroos, koalas and rabbits.*)

---

[1] Learners of English as an Additional Language/English as a Second Language

A functional perspective

The approach to grammar adopted in this book draws heavily upon the pioneering work done by Professor Michael Halliday in the area of Systemic Functional Linguistics. Functional Grammar is built upon a series of assumptions about the way language works in context:

- Language is a dynamic, complex system of resources for making meaning.
- Language reflects the culture in which it has evolved. It is not a neutral medium, but expresses certain world views, values, beliefs and attitudes.
- Our language choices change from situation to situation, depending on the social purpose for which language is being used, the subject matter, who is involved, and whether the language is spoken or written.
- The emphasis in language study is on how people use authentic language in various contexts in real life to achieve their purposes. The particular focus of this book will be on the language needed for successful participation in school contexts.
- A knowledge of grammar can help us to critically evaluate our own texts and those of others (eg identifying point of view; examining how language can be manipulated to achieve certain effects and position the reader in different ways; knowing how language can be used to construct various identities or a particular way of viewing the world).

A functional approach looks at how language enables us to do things in our daily lives. To participate successfully in school and the community, for example, students need to know how to use language:

- for achieving different social purposes
- for sharing ideas about their experience of the world
- for making connections between these ideas
- for interacting with others
- and for constructing coherent texts in both spoken and written modes.

Achieving different social purposes

As they progress through school and life, learners need to be able to use language in order to achieve a range of social purposes such as describing, explaining, arguing or recounting. These different social purposes are expressed through different text types (or genres). Young children operate with a moderate range of text types, which generally have a relatively basic, unelaborated structure (eg recounts involving only a couple of events, arguments that are often unsupported by evidence, explanations of only a sentence or two in length). With teacher guidance over the years, students should be able to confidently interpret and employ a wide range of text types for a variety of social purposes, including texts that have a more complex, unpredictable structure. This provides students with a solid preparation for the demands of secondary school and life in the community.

The *Australian Curriculum: English* requires that students develop proficiency in a range of text types for a variety of purposes. While not dealing in detail with different text types, this book will refer to how different grammatical resources are drawn on in achieving different social purposes, such as the use of the past tense to refer to events in a recount or the use of the present tense to refer to 'timeless' actions in an information report.

Expressing ideas

A major function of language is to represent experience, to help us to express and understand what goes on in our lives. This is sometimes called the 'observer' function of language. In the school context, this includes using and understanding the language of the different areas of the curriculum. It is now well known that each disciplinary area has its own way of using language to develop knowledge and understandings relevant to that area. The language of science, for example, is quite different from the language of history. The language used in English literary texts is quite different from that of geography texts. Students need to be able to read and write texts that become increasingly technical, abstract, and subject-specific as they move through the school system from primary to secondary school.

On entering school, students' language will be concerned with more particular, everyday understandings ('my family', 'our neighbourhood'). As they grow older, they need to be able to talk and write in more generalised terms ('families', 'dinosaurs') about less familiar topics which often require research ('the planets', 'volcanic eruptions') and specialist terminology ('solar system', 'lava'). It cannot be taken for granted that this type of language will develop automatically.

Chapter 2 illustrates how grammar functions to represent experience: the kinds of activities taking place; the participants in those activities; and the circumstances surrounding those activities.

Connecting ideas

Not only do students need to know how to express ideas through language, they need to make connections between ideas. Simple connections can be made by using words such as *and*, *but* and *so*. However, if students are to be able to comprehend and produce more complex connections between ideas, they will need to deal with more sophisticated ways of reasoning and creating logical relationships through language. Knowing how to construct and interpret lengthy sentences that contain a number of ideas in complex relationships is a skill that continues to develop throughout secondary school.

Chapter 3 deals with the various ways in which ideas can be connected to make richer sentences.

Interacting with others

Another major function of language is to enable interaction. Through language we construct particular roles and relationships. Students need to be able to use language effectively to interact with a range of people. In the early years, they will use language in more informal, familiar ways with known peers and adults, freely expressing their feelings and attitudes. Gradually they will also need to learn ways of expressing themselves that are a bit more formal and detached, with a more subtle use of evaluative language and modality, particularly in the written mode.

In school, children need the skills of group interaction, the ability to take part in class discussions, the poise to talk with both familiar and unfamiliar adults. They need to know how to cope in situations with different degrees of authority and power. They need to know how to take on an expanding range of roles: group leader; observer; apprentice; mediator; initiator; questioner; co-learner. They need to be able to evaluate their own interaction skills and to reflect critically on the ways in which others use language to interact with them in oral and written language (eg Are they being persuaded to accept a particular point of view? How is language being used to do this? How might they recognise this and resist if necessary?). In many cases, children will need explicit assistance in developing these interpersonal skills.

Chapter 4 looks at how different grammatical categories are involved when making statements, asking questions, giving commands, expressing opinions, making judgements and engaging with others.

Creating coherent and cohesive texts

Finally, language functions to create texts that are cohesive and coherent. One of the major shifts in children's language use over the primary years is from the spoken mode to the written mode. When students enter school, they are accustomed to using language in face-to-face oral interaction. It is spontaneous and immediate. It generally refers to the 'here-and-now' and to the surrounding context. There is a conversation partner who can provide support by asking questions, giving feedback, and requesting clarification. When moving to the written mode, students need to learn how to use language in quite different ways. Texts will involve a degree of planning, revising and reworking and will therefore be more highly structured. Because the writer has more time to construct the text, the sentences are generally more 'crafted', with greater complexity and density. And because a written text needs to be able to stand on its own, the reader cannot get help from an interaction partner or the surrounding setting. The reader must use cues from the text itself to understand how it is developing. The writer needs to know how to guide the reader through the text. This involves quite sophisticated language skills (eg using the beginning of the sentence and paragraphs to indicate how the topic is developing, using text connectives, and compacting information so that it does not sound rambling). Moving successfully from spoken to written modes is one of the major achievements of primary schooling, requiring the development of a number of high-level skills and strategies. Even in secondary school, however, the ability to create and comprehend highly complex texts continues to develop.

Chapter 5 deals with the ways in which texts are shaped in ways that make them more cohesive and coherent.

Texts in context

The language choices we make are influenced by the context: the purpose, field, tenor and mode.

The **social purpose** for which we use language impacts on our choice of **genre/text type** and the way in which the genre unfolds in characteristic stages to achieve its purpose. If the social purpose, for example, is to tell what happened, the typical choice of genre would be a recount. A recount will generally begin with an 'Orientation' stage in which the various participants are introduced and the time and setting clarified. This is followed by a 'Record of Events', outlining what happened in chronological order. An exposition, on the other hand, will typically begin with a 'Statement of Position', outlining the proposal being argued for. This will be followed by a series of supporting 'Arguments' which are brought together in the 'Conclusion'.[2]

The **field** being developed – 'What is the subject-matter?' – will influence our language choices for **expressing and connecting ideas** (the 'ideational' function of language). If the field, for example, involves providing information about different types of rocks, then our language choices would probably include technical, generalised, descriptive noun groups (***most igneous rocks*** *are* ***silicate minerals***) and relating verbs in the present tense (*Sedimentary rocks* ***are*** *less abundant.*) Ideas might be connected in a causal relationship: <u>*Sedimentary rocks are formed*</u> *x* <u>*by tiny grains of material pressing against each other.*</u>

The **tenor** of the context – 'Who is involved in the interaction?' – will influence our language choices for **interacting with others** (the 'interpersonal' function of language). Here we are concerned with how the roles being taken up (husband/ wife; teacher/student; doctor/patient; shopkeeper/customer) and the relationships between people (intimate, familiar, distant or infrequent) affect the ways in which we interact through language. Factors such as age, gender, authority, expertise, and class can also play a part, as can the degree to which the context is 'interpersonally charged'.

The **mode** – 'What is the channel of communication?' – will influence our language choices when we are **creating cohesive and coherent texts** (the 'textual' function of language). The free-flowing, spontaneous language of spoken texts, for example, is quite different from the compact, carefully crafted language of written texts.

Any particular combination of field, tenor and mode in a situation is referred to as the 'register'. By being aware of the genre and register, we are able to predict the language choices that would be typical of that situation. We can represent the relationship between the context and language system in the following diagram:

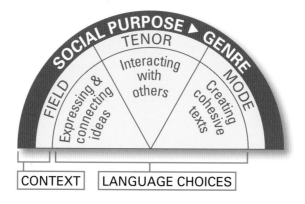

---

2   The various ways in which text types are structured have been described elsewhere, for example *Exploring How Texts Work* (PETA 1990).

Language and learning

The following table summarises how the different language functions are involved in students' learning through the years of school.

EARLY YEARS	LATER YEARS

LANGUAGE FOR ACHIEVING DIFFERENT PURPOSES

Producing and comprehending a small range of text types with basic structures for specific purposes.	Producing and interpreting a wide range of text types for varied social purposes, with more complex structures (multiple purposes, 'hybrids' (eg *infomercials*), and less predictable stages).

LANGUAGE FOR REPRESENTING EXPERIENCE

Dealing with everyday, familiar, individualised, concrete, non-specialised subject matter, represented by non-elaborated noun groups, simple verb groups using a limited range of tenses, and a basic selection of adverbials (primarily *when, where* and *how*).	Dealing with more technical, generalised, abstract, discipline-specific subject matter, represented by richly elaborated noun groups, complex verb groups using a broad range of tenses and aspects, and an extensive variety of adverbials expressing the circumstances surrounding the activity.

LANGUAGE FOR CONNECTING IDEAS

Linking ideas in simple, spoken-like manner, using connectors such as *and, but* and *so*.	Creating more complex connections between ideas and managing the development of lengthy, well-structured sentences containing a variety of clause types.

LANGUAGE FOR INTERACTING WITH OTHERS

Operating in contexts that involve more personal interaction with known individuals; a limited range of roles; freely expressed emotions; evaluations grounded in personal opinion not necessarily supported by evidence.	Operating in contexts which include more impersonal, formal, interaction with a wide range of individuals and groups – both familiar and unfamiliar; expanded range of roles; more nuanced expression of emotion; more detached and informed appreciation and judgement, grounded in explicit criteria and supported by evidence; discerning use of intensifiers; careful use of modality and other resources to create spaces for alternative perspectives and possibilities; critical awareness of how language can be used to position self and others.

LANGUAGE FOR CREATING COHERENT AND COHESIVE TEXTS

Participating in face-to-face, spontaneous, context-dependent dialogues; engaging with relatively brief written texts involving minimal use of cohesive resources.	Engaging with texts that are monologic, crafted and planned, and independent of the immediate context; comprehending and producing lengthy, cohesive texts that require careful organisation and guidance of the reader.

Terminology

In all contemporary grammars of English, there are terms that relate to the grammatical class (eg noun) and terms that relate to the functions that such a grammatical category can perform (eg Participant in an activity[3]). This is important, as each grammatical category can do a variety of jobs. There is no one-to-one correspondence between form and function. An adverb, for example, can tell about the circumstances surrounding an activity (*quickly*), or it can express a particular viewpoint (*unfortunately*), or it can intensify (*very*), or it can indicate the strength of commitment (*probably*), or it can help to make links within a text (*firstly*), and so on.

In this edition, there is greater detail in terms of the two kinds of terminology. Ideally, students should be familiar both with terms that refer to form (eg noun group, verb group) and terms that refer to their functions (eg Participant, Process). Some teachers, particularly when focusing on meaning, might choose to work just with the functional terms – especially when students are first learning about grammar. Others, particularly when focusing on form and structure, might use the formal terms. Ultimately, it is a matter of what students already know about grammar, how that knowledge can be extended in ways that are productive, and how the knowledge about language is built over the years, preferably through whole-school planning for teaching and learning.

Over the centuries, different terminology has developed as our understanding about language has evolved. In many cases, different terms are in circulation, depending on the particular description of English and when it was in use. In this book, footnotes have been used to indicate when a particular language feature might be referred to using different terms.

Links to the *Australian Curriculum: English*

The current edition has been substantially revised in order to provide support to teachers as they implement the national curriculum – and in particular the Knowledge about Language strand. The organisation of the Language strand reflects the three major functions of language: 'Interacting with others' (the Interpersonal function); 'text structure and organisation' (the Textual function); and 'expressing and developing ideas' (the Ideational function). The terminology used here is very similar to that in the national curriculum, though it might vary slightly in certain instances.

Throughout this edition, relevant Content Descriptions and Elaborations from the English curriculum have been included. These are shaded in blue. The Elaborations are distinguished by the use of a dot point.

Considerations for teaching grammar

Most children will learn how to use grammar implicitly by engaging in extensive and purposeful talking, listening, reading, writing and viewing. Children – including those from language backgrounds other than English – come to school with

---

[3] A capital letter is often used for functional terms.

a highly-developed ability to use language in rich and complex ways. Their language will continue to develop as they use it for a variety of purposes in their homes, in the community and school. In addition to learning language through social interaction, this book will assume that the teacher plays a deliberate role in enhancing children's use of language and in developing their knowledge about language.

Learning to ...

In the classroom, students will be learning to use language in particular ways. The teacher's role is to design contexts and plan activities in all curriculum areas that provide opportunities for learners to develop the particular language they need in order to participate effectively in school. The teacher's knowledge about language will assist in selecting resources, choosing texts, focusing on salient points, constructing language-rich activities, responding to questions, assessing students' work, and providing informed feedback. At the end of various sections of this book, you will find a section on how teachers might monitor the development of particular language features at various stages of development. This is not intended as an assessment tool, but rather as an indication of directions in which teachers might actively promote students' language use.

The teacher plays an important role in modelling and promoting the use of Standard Australian English – particularly for students from language backgrounds other than English or students whose home language is not closely aligned with the language of the school. While respecting and appreciating the diverse language backgrounds of all the students in the class, the teacher has a responsibility to explicitly and systematically apprentice learners into the language of the school.

Learning about ...

In addition to fostering children's ability to use language in particular ways, the teacher can tap into the learner's implicit knowledge about language and help make it more explicit. The teacher can provide learners with tools for reflecting on how language works. Together they build up a shared language for talking about language (a 'metalanguage') so that they can refer to the various functions and structures of language. During activities such as shared and guided reading, modelled and collaborative writing, conferencing, and in class discussions, the teacher is able to focus on how language is functioning. By selecting certain texts, focusing on relevant features, highlighting specific points, and asking particular questions, the teacher draws students' attention to ways in which language is being used. In this way the teacher is able to demonstrate how grammar is contributing to the meaning of the text.

Grammar should generally be taught in the context of working with whole texts (eg identifying grammatical patterns that help a particular text type achieve its purpose). The emphasis should not be on the ability simply to label a particular feature, but on its usefulness in creating, appreciating and evaluating texts. Students should be shown how grammar helps to build up the meaning of the text. When dealing with information reports, for example, the teacher might want to demonstrate how the timeless present tense is used for generalising. This can then be contrasted with the specific past tense actions found in recounts. The texts used when teaching grammar should be authentic, not artificial and contrived simply to teach a grammatical point. They may, however, need to be simplified, when first introducing a certain feature.

There are times, however, when it might be more efficient to look at a particular, relevant aspect of grammar more intensively. For example, if a specific feature is presenting particular challenges, then additional language activities on that feature could be explored, using a number of clear examples taken from texts.

Certain groups of students will need more systematic and focused assistance with particular features of English grammar, eg students from language backgrounds other than English. Emphasis should be placed on the construction of clear, well-formed, and coherent sentences and texts, and not so much on the rules of usage (eg whether to finish a sentence with a preposition, whether to use *will* or *shall*.)

Teachers need to use their own judgement as to how much information or detail the students can usefully and comfortably deal with at any particular time. The grammatical features outlined in this book should serve as a guide as to what might reasonably be learned by most children during the years of schooling.

The study of grammar need not be onerous or dry. There is room for playfulness and creativity, for experimentation and discovery, for enjoyment and wonder. Children have an instinctive fascination with language. It is the teacher's job to nurture this.

Levels of language

When we are teaching about language, we need to be clear about which level we are dealing with.

Text

Modern linguists now recognise that language patterns extend beyond the sentence and can operate at the level of the whole text. At the text level, we find patterns that are related to a particular text type (eg the use of commands in a procedure, action verbs in a recount, abstract nouns in an exposition, dialogue in a narrative). We also find certain features that serve to link parts of a text: cohesive devices such as pronouns; words that create relationships within the text (eg synonyms, repeated words); words that signal how the text is structured (eg *Firstly* ... ; *On the one hand* ...). In achieving its purpose, the language patterns change as the text moves through its various stages. When introducing the characters in a story, for example, we find long descriptive noun groups. When the text moves to an action sequence, the emphasis is on action verbs. And when there is a reflective stage, there will be more thinking and feeling verbs.

Sentence

A text is made up of a number of sentences. Sentences can consist of a single clause or a number of clauses joined together. Students need to know how to combine clauses to make sentences and how to construct different types of relationships between clauses in a sentence (eg relationships of time, place, causality and concession).

Clause

A clause is a unit of meaning that expresses a message. It typically contains a verb/verb group. The clause is often seen as the basic unit for analysing language.

Group/Phrase

A clause consists of smaller 'chunks' or groups of words that do certain jobs. In the clause *a group of small children were digging in the sand*, the core of the clause is the verb group (eg ***were digging***). Participating in this action might be one or more persons or things, represented by a noun group (eg **A group of small children** *were digging*). There might also be some extra information in the form of an adverbial (eg *A group of small children were digging* **in the sand**).

Word

Groups and phrases can be divided into individual words. In a noun group, for example, we might find an article, an adjective and a noun (eg *the wily fox*). It is important to see how individual words function within a group so that students can see how the words relate to each other.

In the past, grammar was often taught at the level of the individual word, eg 'noun', 'verb', 'preposition'. While these categories are important, students often ended up with a fragmented knowledge of the system, with little idea of how these words work together to make meaning or how different shades of meanings could be made through author choices.

| **TEXT LEVEL** (excerpt) | Alice caught the baby with some difficulty, as it was a queer-shaped little creature, and held out its arms and legs in all directions, 'just like a star-fish,' thought Alice. The poor little thing was snorting like a steam-engine when she caught it. It kept doubling itself up and straightening itself out again, so that altogether, for the first minute or two, it was as much as she could do to hold it. |

| **SENTENCE LEVEL** | The poor little thing was snorting like a steam-engine | when she caught it. |

| **CLAUSE LEVEL** | The poor little thing was snorting like a steam-engine |

| **GROUP/PHRASE LEVEL** | The poor little thing | was snorting | like a steam-engine |

| **WORD LEVEL** | The | poor | little | thing | was | snorting | like | a | steam-engine |

2 Language for expressing ideas

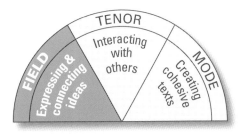

One important function of language is to enable us to represent what is going on in the world: to talk about our experiences, to reflect on our observations, to share knowledge and ideas.[1] Here we are concerned with how we use language to create different 'worlds': literary, imaginative, mathematical, scientific, historical or everyday.

A key resource for observing the world is the clause – the basic unit of meaning. Clauses do many different jobs. In terms of representing the world, a clause provides information about what is going on, who/what is taking part, and any circumstances surrounding the activity (When? Where? How? etc).

Recognise that sentences are key units for expressing ideas [Foundation]

We could say that a clause represents a slice of experience.

Where?	Who/what is taking part?	What's happening?	How?'
In the treetop	*the cat*	*was smiling*	*mysteriously.*
CLAUSE			

In representing experience, each part of the clause has a different function.

One of the best ways of introducing students to a new grammatical feature is to use a 'probe question', which draws their attention to the meaning or function of the feature. When exploring the clause and its parts, for example, it is useful to start by using probe questions such as:

---

[1] While 'language for expressing ideas' captures the intention of this chapter to a certain extent, it is more broadly concerned with how language functions to represent difference kinds of experience. Halliday refers to this as the 'experiential' or 'ideational' function of language.

What is happening?

Who or what is taking part?

What gives us more information about the activity? When? Where? How? etc

Identify the parts of a simple sentence that represent 'What's happening?', 'Who or what is doing or receiving the action?' and circumstances surrounding the action [Year 1]

This will help the students to start thinking in terms of 'chunks of meaning' rather than individual words. When students use one of these questions to find a clause part, and to identify its function, they can use functional terms to describe its meaning (eg What kind of Process is taking place?; Who/What is the Participant in this activity?; What kind of Circumstance is this?). When discussing the grammatical forms used to express these functions, students can use formal terms (eg verb group, noun group or adverb).[2]

	Where?	Who/what is taking part?	What's happening?	How?
	In the treetop	the cat	was smiling	mysteriously.
MEANING	Circumstance	Participant	Process	Circumstance
FORM	↘ prepositional phrase[3]	↘ noun group	↘ verb group	↘ adverb
CLAUSE				

Explore differences in words that represent people, places and things (nouns and pronouns), actions (verbs), qualities (adjectives) and details like when, where and how (adverbs) [Year 1]

■ knowing that, in terms of meaning, a basic clause represents: what is happening (verb); who or what is participating (noun group); and the surrounding circumstances (adverbial) [Year 1]

When introducing students to grammar from a functional perspective, it is not always a matter of whether something is 'right' or 'wrong' but whether students find the metalanguage useful for exploring the meaning of the text. Sometimes there are blurred edges when we talk about meaning and students should be encouraged to have lively discussions about the meaning and function of a particular linguistic feature.

Understand that a clause is a unit of meaning [Year 3]

■ knowing that a clause is basically a group of words that contains a verb [Year 3]

---

[2] It is not a matter of 'meaning' or 'form' but of how different meanings are expressed by different forms. Grammar always looks two ways – towards form and towards meaning.
[3] A sloping arrow is often used to mean 'is expressed by'. For example, the meaning 'Participant' is typically expressed (or 'realised') by a noun group.

and we **sway**

in a dare-devil way

on a hair-raising,

zig-zagging track.

Our father

once **tried.**

You'll **find** him

inside

with a very

large bruise

on his back.[9]

Max Fatchen

Not all action verbs represent physical activities. Sometimes they are relatively abstract.

*'Can you **manage** all right?'*

*She **retained** her sense of humour.*

*He couldn't **provide** a good reason.*

*Outbreaks of violence **occurred** frequently.*

*The inflation rate **has increased** lately.*

There is also a group similar to action verbs that are sometimes referred to as 'behavioural processes'. These tend to represent (typically human) bodily actions usually only with one participant (eg *stare, listen, worry, dream, breathe, sneeze, cough, hiccup, burp, faint, yawn, sleep, cry, laugh, smile, frown, sigh, sob, snarl, chatter, grumble, gossip, argue,* and *whine*). They often lie between 'doing' and 'sensing' but for our purposes, this finer distinction might not be necessary.

Saying verbs

Sometimes experience is not represented directly, but is reported verbally. The following are some common saying verbs:[10]

saying verbs				
ask	deny	plead	respond	stammer
claim	explain	promise	say	suggest
continue	imply	reply	scream	tell
cry	murmur	report	shout	whisper

---

[9] Note that there are also parts of this text where action words are used as 'describers': breathtaking trip; hair-raising; zig-zagging track. There are also instances where actions have been represented as 'things': a shove; a run; a sweep; a swerve. These no longer have the form of verbs but retain the meaning of an action.

[10] These are called Verbal Processes in Hallidayan grammar.

■ exploring action and saying verbs in narrative texts to show how they give information about what characters do and say [Year 3]

You can generally test whether a verb is potentially a 'saying verb' by asking whether it can be followed by items such as 'that', 'whether' or 'what':[11]

She promised **that** she would come back.

She claimed **that** it was a plot.

She explained **what** had been troubling her.

She asked **whether** she could go home.

Another rule of thumb is whether the verb can take a 'receiver':

She promised **him** ...;

She explained **to her mother** ...;

She asked **the teacher** ...

Saying verbs are found most commonly in stories, where we get to know the characters by the way they speak and interact with others. In the following passage, for example, J.K. Rowling could have simply said that Dudley was a belligerent, spoilt child, but instead she gives an insight into his personality through the choice of saying verbs:

> "Make it move," he **whined** at his father. Uncle Vernon tapped on the glass, but the snake didn't budge.
> "Do it again," Dudley **ordered**. Uncle Vernon rapped the glass smartly with his knuckles, but the snake just snoozed on.
> "This is boring," Dudley **moaned**. He shuffled away.
>
> *Harry Potter and the Sorcerer's Stone*, J.K. Rowling

In shared reading, students could explore the different saying verbs used (eg pleaded, whispered, responded, sighed) and discuss how these can be more effective than *said*. Students could be asked to read the lines aloud in the manner suggested by the saying verb: *'Don't hit me!'*; he *blubbered/stammered/croaked/hissed/whimpered*. They could also look at the manner expressions[12] used with saying verbs that help to build up the character and mood (eg *severely, humbly, angrily, in a languid, sleepy voice, rather eagerly, in a soothing tone*). Students could contribute to wordbanks of saying verbs to refer to later in their own writing.

Saying verbs are also important in newspaper articles, where it is reported what people *said (promised, threatened, implied* or *announced)*. This could become part of a media study unit (eg involving a critical evaluation of how people's 'sayings' are interpreted, quoted or reported).

When looking at saying verbs, we can also deal with such matters as the difference between direct and indirect speech, and the punctuation of direct speech.[13]

---

[11] Though this will depend on context. Note, for example, the difference between 'He screamed that he was hungry' (saying verb) and 'The baby didn't stop screaming' (action/behavioural verb).

[12] See Circumstances of manner, p. 67

[13] See section on Quoting and Reporting, page 97.

Sensing verbs

Sensing verbs[14] reflect processes of our 'internal world'. They are typically used only in relation to humans – or non-humans given human-like qualities – describing what they think, feel, desire and perceive. The following are some examples:

thinking		feeling and wanting	perceiving
know	decide	like	see
reflect	consider	hate	taste
comprehend	recall	dislike	hear
believe	hypothesise	want	smell
imagine	wonder	wish	observe
forget	understand	need	notice
remember	assume	fear	sense
recollect	recognise	enjoy	
realise	infer		

■ exploring the use of sensing verbs and how they allow readers to know what characters think and feel [Year 3]

As with saying verbs, the students can test whether a verb is a sensing verb by asking whether it can potentially be followed by 'that':

> She understood **that** ...

> She noticed **that** ...

> She forgot **that** ...

As this isn't always the case (eg *She understood what it meant*; *She understood his concern*.) another test is to ask about the tense. A sensing verb will usually take a simple tense (*She forgot ...*) rather than a progressive (*She was forgetting ...*).

In a story, sensing verbs can give us insight into the characters of a story by describing what is going on in their minds. They are often used when characters reflect on the action or evaluate what is happening in the story.

> "But then," **thought** Alice, "shall I never get any older than I am now? That'll be a comfort, one way – never to be an old woman – but then – always to have lessons to **learn**! Oh, **I shouldn't like** that!" ... But a few minutes later she **heard** a voice outside. "Mary Ann! Mary Ann!" said the voice. "Fetch me my gloves this moment!" Then came a little pattering of feet on the stairs. Alice **knew** it was the Rabbit coming to look for her, and she trembled till she shook the house, quite **forgetting** that she was now a thousand times as large as the Rabbit and had no reason to be afraid of it."
>
> Lewis Carroll

---

14 Halliday refers to these as Mental Processes.

Thinking verbs are used to express processes of cognition and can feature in texts such as arguments and discussions (eg *It is thought that ...; I believe that ...; I wonder whether ...*) where we are interested in people's ideas and opinions or in stories where a character is reflecting:

> This is a hospital, he **thought**. I am in a hospital. But he **could remember** nothing. He lay back on his pillow, looking at the ceiling and **wondering** what had happened. He was gazing at the smooth greyness of the ceiling which was so clean and grey, and then suddenly he saw a fly walking upon it. The sight of this fly, the suddenness of seeing this small black speck on a sea of grey, brushed the surface of his brain, and quickly, in that second, he **remembered** everything. He **remembered** the Spitfire and he **remembered** the altimeter showing twenty-one thousand feet. He **remembered** the pushing back of the hood with both hands, and he **remembered** the bailing out. He **remembered** his leg.
>
> *Beware of the Dog*, R. Dahl

Sensing verbs are concerned not only with people's thoughts but with their feelings and desires. We often find people expressing their emotions in texts such as romance novels, poems, songs and blogs:

> ### *Why I hate sports*
>
> I'm just going to come right out and say it. I **hate** all sports. Even the ones I sometimes **like**. Now this is, of course, downright unAustralian of me so I'm going to try to defend my position. First of all, you **need** to know that I **enjoy** physical activity. But what I **loathe** is the brittle rhetoric that surrounds almost all sporting endeavour. The forum in which I **resent** this rhetoric the most is children's sports. Why do we make children who aren't naturally good at sport race their classmates in front of huge audiences? The kid who comes last doesn't get a trophy but sits in the great silent stillness of the non-winner, feeling like a loser.
>
> *Adapted from http://fantasticthoughts.wordpress.com /2009/10/19/why-i-hate-sports/*

Sensing verbs also encompass actions of perception – those that involve the use of our senses: seeing, hearing, tasting, and smelling.

> He **heard** the cows mooing loudly
> As they invaded the vegie garden.
>
> He **saw** the herd devouring his sage and thyme
> As they trampled the artichokes.
>
> He **felt** his chest thumping
> as he chased them into the barn.
>
> He **smelled** the beef roasting
> As he stoked the sizzling coals.
>
> He **tasted** the flavour of freshly herbed steak
> As he savoured the thought of a moo-free morning.

Relating verbs

There are some verbs that do not represent actions, speaking, thoughts or feelings. Their job is to simply link two pieces of information.

| Alice | was | now more than nine feet tall. |

We can call these 'relating verbs'.[15] The most common relating verbs are the verbs *be* and *have* and variations on these.

being		having
am, is, are, was, were mean become turn into seem appear	represent remain is called equal symbolise	have, has, had possess own include comprise lack encompass

- exploring the use of relating verbs in constructing definitions and descriptions [Year 3]

In some cases, a link is being made between the thing being described and its description:

Thing being described	Relating verb	Description
The Bloodbottler	*was*	*a gruesome sight.*
The girls	*became*	*close friends.*
The sky	*grew*	*darker.*
Rudolph	*had*	*a very shiny nose.*
Eagles	*possess*	*strong beaks.*
He	*seems*	*happy enough.*
Anzac Cove	*was*	*a bloody scene of putrid corpses, extreme weather and appalling health conditions.*

In other cases, the link is between a thing and how it is being identified or defined:

Thing being identified	Relating verb	Identifier
A bat	*is*	*the only mammal that can fly.*
The land	*is symbolised by*	*the colour red.*
A solid	*refers to*	*a figure having three dimensions.*

---

[15] These are also referred to by such terms as Relational Processes and linking verbs.

In the case of a true definition, it is possible to reverse the two Participants:

A sonnet	is	a poem of fourteen lines that follows a strict rhyme scheme and specific structure.
A poem of fourteen lines that follows a strict rhyme scheme and specific structure.	is called	a sonnet.

Note that some of the verbs above appear to be the same as sensing verbs. Generally, however, if they are followed by a describing item (eg using an adjective), they have a relating function, linking something to its description:

> The bread **tastes** stale.

> The flowers **smelled** divine.

> I **felt** sore all over.

> It **looked** suspicious.

It is important to remember that a word (or group of words) can have a different function depending on the context.

Existing verbs

Another type of verb is where there is no action or relationship being described, simply a state:

> **There was** an old house on the hill.

> **There is** a hole in your jeans.

> **There are** no decent shows on television.

> **There was** nothing to do.

> **There was** not a breath of air stirring.

These are typically introduced by there.[16]

> Down below **there was** only a vast white undulating sea of cloud. Above **there was** the sun, and the sun was white like the clouds, because it is never yellow when one looks at it from high in the air. ...
>
> He glanced down again at his right leg. **There was** not much of it left. ...
>
> He knew then that he must bail out; that **there was** not a second to lose, otherwise he would become unconscious. ...
>
> **There were** some roses on the table by his bed. Then he saw the basin on the table near the roses. It was a white enamel basin, and beside it **there was** a small medicine glass. ...
>
> He saw a small house with a grey tiled roof standing alone beside a narrow lane, and immediately behind it **there was** a ploughed field.

---

[16] In this case 'there' refers to the existence of something, not a place.

> In front of the house **there <u>was</u>** an untidy garden, and **there <u>was</u>** a green hedge separating the garden from the lane. He was looking at the hedge when he saw the sign. ... **There <u>was</u>** something written on the board with white paint ... **There <u>were</u>** three words ...

Beware of the Dog, R. Dahl

Looking at form: The verb group

In representing processes, we use the verb group. A verb group can consist of a single word (eg He **wrote** a letter.) or a number of words (eg He **might have been going to write** a letter.). We refer to a verb by using its base form (eg come, read, eat). The base form typically provides the 'content' of the verb – 'What's going on?'.

Verb groups help to locate an action or state in time through the use of tense.[17] The two main tenses of English are the simple present tense and the simple past tense. These tenses are formed simply by using or changing the base form.

Understand that processes are anchored in time through tense [Year 3]

■ learning how time is represented through the tense of a verb and other structural, language and visual features [Year 3]

The simple present tense

The simple present tense typically involves a single word (eg *walk/s*) and is formed by using the base form of the verb – but adds an **-s** (or **-es**) for *he, she* and *it*.

base form		
want	I, you, we, they **want**	he, she, it **wants**
go	I, you, we, they **go**	he, she, it **goes**
watch	I, you, we, they **watch**	he, she, it **watches**

TROUBLESHOOTING

1 When adding **-es** to the base form of some verbs, adjustments need to be made, eg: *hurry* ▶ *hurries*.

2 Remembering to add the **-s** (or **-es**) can cause a problem for learners of English, especially at the beginner level.

3 Two of the most common verbs in English – *be* and *have* – are irregular in the present tense, another potential issue for English learners:

base form	
be	I **am**, you **are**, he/she/it **is**, we **are**, they **are**
have	I **have**, you **have**, he/she/it **has**, we **have**, they **have**

---

[17] The intent here is to provide students with a basic introduction to the notion of 'tense'. If a more detailed discussion would be of interest to your students, these are readily available online and in other grammar books.

The simple present tense can be used to indicate a variety of perspectives on time:

meaning	simple present tense
right now/commentary	*Here they come!* *He knows what I mean.*
on-going states	*She is in Grade 2.*
habitual actions	*I clean my teeth every day.*
timeless	*The planets orbit the sun.*
referring to the future (if scheduled activity)	*They leave on Sunday.*
referring to the past when narrating in dramatic fashion ('historical present')	*And then he just hits me for no reason.*

■ knowing that the simple present tense is typically used to talk about actions that happen regularly in the present (for example 'He watches TV every night.') or that represent 'timeless' actions, as in information reports (for example 'Bears hibernate in winter.') [Year 6]

The simple past tense

The simple past tense is typically formed by adding **-ed** to the base form.

base form	
want	I, you, he/she/it, we, they **wanted**
talk	I, you, he/she/it, we, they **talked**

■ knowing the difference between the simple present tense (for example 'Pandas eat bamboo.') and the simple past tense (for example 'She replied.') [Year 6]

TROUBLESHOOTING

When adding **-ed** to the base form of some verbs, adjustments need to be made, eg: *worry* ▶ *worried; flap* ▶ *flapped.*

Many verbs, however, are irregular in the past tense:

base form	irregular simple past tense
go	went
buy	bought
have	had
be	was, were
come	came
say	said
see	saw
do	did

Past tense irregularities cause major problems for learners of English, particularly as many of the commonly used verbs are irregular.

As with the simple present tense, the simple past tense can be used to represent a variety of perspectives on time:

meaning	simple past tense
point in time	Shakespeare **died** in 1616.
on-going states in the past	They **were** my favourite toys.
habitual actions in the past	We **wrote** to each other daily.
hypothesising	If they **studied** hard they would pass the test.
politeness	I **wondered** whether you would like to come.

Other aspects of time

Apart from the simple present and the simple past, the verb group provides us with resources to be quite specific about various aspects[18] of time. While students need not be explicitly taught all the information below (unless, of course, they are interested or studying another language), teachers should be familiar with the main points in order to identify potential problems in students' use of verb forms and to expand students' ability to express and comprehend more precise and subtle meanings regarding time.

The 'progressive' aspect, for example, allows us to specify an on-going action that is unfinished, incomplete or only temporary: He **is studying** French; they **were discussing** the problem. In this case, the verb group consists of an auxiliary[19] and a participle:

VERB GROUP	
auxiliary ('be')	-ing participle[20]
is	studying
were	discussing
was	talking

The auxiliary in this case is the present or past tense of the verb be. Typically, the function of the auxiliary is to locate the action in time (is vs. was). The auxiliary agrees with the Subject (he **was** talking vs. we **were** talking).

The participle in this case is the base form of the verb plus **-ing**. The participle retains the 'content meaning' of the verb (eg studying, running, dreaming).

---

[18] The term 'aspect' is being used here rather loosely. For a more technical discussion of tense and aspect, you can consult a more detailed grammar reference book.
[19] Auxiliaries are often referred to as 'helping verbs' in primary years.
[20] This is sometimes called the 'present participle'.

Sometimes we refer to a progressive action that was interrupted by another action:

*While she **was talking**, Ibrahim **walked in**.*

The progressive can also be used to refer to an action in the future:

*We **are going** to the zoo tomorrow.*

The 'perfect' aspect refers to an event in the past that is finished or complete but that relates to a subsequent event. If we say, for example, *They have gone to the movies*, there is an expectation that they will be coming back later. Compare this with *They went to the movies* – an event over and done. The verb group again consists of an auxiliary and a participle, but this time the auxiliary is the verb 'have' and the participle is an **-ed** participle.[21]

VERB GROUP	
auxiliary ('have')	**-ed participle**
has	walked
have	discussed
had	hoped

A major problem here is that many **-ed** participles are irregular. Several end in **-en** (*he has spok**en**; they have driv**en**; she has eat**en***). Others are quite unpredictable:

base form	irregular participle
go	*they have **gone***
do	*I had **done***
bring	*we have **brought***
put	*she has **put***
teach	*you had **taught***
be	*it has **been***
came	*they had **come***
say	*you have **said***

---

[21] This is sometimes called the 'past participle'. Note that not all past participles end in *-ed*.

TROUBLESHOOTING

1 Irregular participles can cause difficulties for learners of English.

2 In informal spoken language, sometimes the participle is used instead of the simple past tense, eg: *He **done** it; they **been** there; he **come** home; I **seen** her*. This is not an issue in casual conversation with peers, family and the community, but might need some work if it appears in students' written school texts.

Other auxiliaries

Modal auxiliaries

Apart from auxiliaries that locate an action in time (*they **are** playing; we **were** driving; he **has** gone; it **had** rained*), there are auxiliaries that function to indicate the degree of certainty surrounding an activity.[22] These are called 'modal' auxiliaries. Here is a list of verb groups consisting of modal auxiliaries plus the base form:

modal auxiliary	base form
might	enrol
must	read
would	consider
could	see
should	leave
may	notice
can	do

VERB GROUP

There are other auxiliaries that aren't strictly modals, but which perform similar functions: *you **need** to pay; they **have** to leave; we **ought** to visit her; we **had better** hurry; we didn't **dare** speak*.

It is possible to find various combinations of elements in the verb group: *we **had been hoping**; they **might have been going to pay**; she **would have seen** it*. Again, it is not necessary that such structures be taught systematically to students. It is important, however, that students be exposed to texts – both spoken and written – where these are used as such forms enable them to make and understand more nuanced, fine-grained meanings.

Understand that the meaning of sentences can be enriched through the use of expanded verb groups [Year 4]

---

[22] See also Chapter 4 (the section on Engagement) for further discussion of modality.

TROUBLESHOOTING

Many young people are not aware of how the verb group is structured and as a result use forms such as 'she would of seen it'. This needs explicit attention.

Future time

Another auxiliary is *will* – generally used to indicate an action in the future as in these sentences from J.R.R. Tolkien's *The Lord of the Rings*:

> He **will** destroy Gondor.
>
> "I**'ll** go with Sam."
>
> Elvish forlorn trees **will** grow there.

■ knowing that there are various ways in English to refer to future time (for example 'She will call you tomorrow'; 'I am going to the movies tomorrow'; 'Tomorrow I leave for Hobart') [Year 6]

Note that there are other ways of referring to the future in English. We can also use the present progressive (*I **am seeing** James on Thursday*), the simple present tense (*We **leave** at six tomorrow*), the form 'be going to' (*I **am going to see** James on Thursday*), or 'be about to' for events in the very near future (*I**'m about** to leave*). This can be a confusing area for ESL students.

Look at how the following poem uses three different verb forms to refer to future time:

> When I **grow up**
>
> I**'m going to be** rich and famous
>
> By inventing the antidote
>
> To the common chocolate.
>
> But until then I**'ll eat** as many as I can
>
> And call it Research.
>
> > Bill Condon

Multi-word verb groups

We often find additional words in the verb group. Sometimes, these are small words such as prepositions and adverbs that are added after the verb:[23]

wake up	sit down	get out	put up with	settle down
get away with	give up on	catch on	turn up	give in

This type of verb group is typically used in informal spoken contexts. When students move into the written mode in educational contexts, they would generally need to use more 'academic' versions:

---

23 These are generally referred to as 'phrasal verbs'.

everyday	formal
get up	rise
give in	concede
put up with	tolerate
head off	depart
find out	ascertain
put off	delay
knock down	defeat
run away	disappear
come in	enter

The everyday forms tend to derive from Anglo-Saxon, which was the language of the home and community, while the academic forms tend to derive from Latin, the language of education and literacy.

Sometimes we need to add a noun to specify the content of the verb group, particularly in combination with verbs such as *give, have, do* and *take*. Again, there are often more formal equivalents:

everyday	formal
have a bath	bathe
do a jig	dance
give a hug	embrace
have a go	attempt

The advantage of the everyday versions is that you can extend the meaning by adding to the noun (*have a **nice hot** bath; give a **long hearty** hug*).

Another way in which we make multi-word verb groups is to include a verb that tells us more about the timing or duration of the action:

> She **_continued_ to cry**.
>
> They **_began_ to climb** *the cliff.*
>
> It **_started_ to rain**.
>
> They **_kept on_ trying**.
>
> He **_finished_ counting** *the beans.*
>
> We **_stopped_ looking**.
>
> *Lehmann's fingers and toes* **_began_ to itch**.

The meaning of the verb group can also be extended by including verbs such as *try, cause, help* or *seem*:

*She **tried** to resist.*

*It **caused** him **to panic**.*

*They **were helping to find out** the truth.*

*He **seemed to be feeling** ill.*

As you can see, the verb group can become quite lengthy:

*He **has been wanting to get started** all morning.*

*Maggie **might have been trying to say** something important.*

Negatives

When we form the negative, we simply add 'not' after the auxiliary:

	auxiliary	'not'	
we	could	**not**	see
he	had	**not**	eaten
she	is	**not**	sleeping
they	might	**not**	notice

But the simple present and simple past tenses do not have auxiliaries. So what can we do? We need to insert an auxiliary, so we use *do*:

simple present and past tenses	auxiliary 'do'	'not'	base verb
he **brought**	did	**not**	bring
she **wants**	does	**not**	want
they **like**	do	**not**	like

Negatives, of course, can be contracted:

They have not remembered. → *They **haven't** remembered.*

We were not doing anything. → *We **weren't** doing anything.*

I do not play the piano. → *I **don't** play the piano.*

He does not like bananas. → *He **doesn't** like bananas.*

She did not work hard. → *She **didn't** work hard.*

They did not come home. → *They **didn't** come home.*

The contraction of the negative in the future tense is irregular:

She will not eat her dinner.   *She **won't** eat her dinner.*

When the process is a 'saying' one, we could refer to the 'sayer' and 'what is said'.[26]

Arwen	whispered	something that made him blanch.
sayer	**saying verb**	**what is said**[27]

Similarly when the activity involves a process of sensing, we find a 'senser' and 'what is sensed':[28]

I	love	the smell of fresh coffee.
The old lady	noticed	something strange.
He	didn't know	the answer.
senser	**sensing verb**	**what is sensed**[29]

When the process is relating two Participants, the types of Participants depend on the kinds of relationships being set up. If, for example, someone or something is being described, one of the participants is 'the person or thing being described' and the other participant is the description. In other words, the 'described' is being related to its 'description':[30]

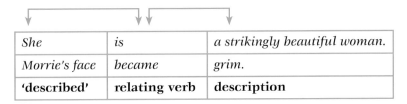

She	is	a strikingly beautiful woman.
Morrie's face	became	grim.
'described'	**relating verb**	**description**

Relating verbs are frequently found in clauses used in information reports and descriptions, where the emphasis is on providing information about something. Being able to read and write clauses that use relating verbs is critical in school learning as it is a major resource for thinking skills such as defining, classifying, exemplifying and describing.

---

[26] Refer to the section on Quoting and Reporting when 'what is said' is a clause.
[27] Technically, 'what is said' is referred to as the Verbiage.
[28] Though, as with saying verbs, see the section on Quoting and Reporting when 'what is sensed' is a clause.
[29] Technically, 'what is sensed' is referred to as the Phenomenon.
[30] Technically, the thing being described is referred to as the Carrier and the description is the Attribute.

Classifying	The kangaroo	is	a type of marsupial.
	thing being classified		**classification**
Defining	Marsupials	are	mammals that raise their young in a pouch.
	technical term		**definition**
Exemplifying	The kangaroo family	includes	kangaroos, wallabies and wallaroos.
	larger group		**examples**
Describing	Kangaroos They	have are	a long tail and strong hind legs. herbivorous.
	thing being described		**description**
Analysing into parts	Kangaroo families	consist of	male kangaroos (boomers or bucks), female kangaroos (does or flyers) and baby kangaroos.
	whole		**parts**
Naming	A baby kangaroo	is called	a joey.
	identified		**identifier**

- Investigate vocabulary typical of extended and more academic texts and the role of abstract nouns, classification, description and generalisation in building specialised knowledge through language [Year 7]

We could summarise these different clause patterns as follows:

do-er	**action verb**	*done-to*
The cat	scratched	my hand.

sayer	**saying verb**	*what is said*
Sam	muttered	something about imperialist oppressors.

senser	**sensing verb**	*what is sensed*
I	remember	your insignificant friend.
They	love	Thai food.
She	wanted	a hug.
He	heard	a commotion from the stables.

entity	**relating verb**	*description/definition/identifier*
Spiders	have	eight legs.
They	are	arachnids.
They	can be	poisonous.

It is often the case that there is only one Participant in a clause (eg **She** sneezed. **They** laughed.). It is also possible to have two Participants (**They** liked **the movie**.) or even three Participants in a clause (**Jim** gave **the dog a bone**. **She** told **him a lie**.)[31]

---

[31] Traditionally, the structure of the clause includes reference to Subject, Direct Object and Indirect Object. If it is considered useful for students to be familiar with such terms, detailed information can be found in most grammar reference books.

By looking at the clause patterns in any text, we can get a feel for how the text is representing the world. In a literary text, for example, we could ask questions such as: Who are the 'do-ers'? What sorts of actions are they involved in? Is anyone or anything generally more passive, in the 'done-to' role? Who is speaking in this text? Why are they chosen to speak? To whom are they speaking? What sorts of things are they saying? Are they being quoted directly or are they being paraphrased? What is the difference in effect? Are the characters portrayed as thinking and feeling beings? What insights do we get into their characters from what they are reported as thinking and feeling? How does this affect the story? What sort of relationship is being set up by the relating verbs (eg description? definition? classification?).

Looking at form: The noun group

Having looked at the kinds of meanings represented by Participants, let's now see how these meanings can be expressed grammatically in the form of a noun group[32] or pronoun. Although we are looking at form, we will continue to refer to meaning and the relationship between form and meaning.

A noun group can consist of a single word (eg *Toad*) or can be expanded to include very lengthy descriptions.

Understand that the meaning of sentences can be enriched through the use of expanded noun groups [Year 4]

Mole and Ratty	*were rowing*	*the tiny wooden boat.*
They	*noticed*	*a handsome, dignified old house of mellowed brick, with well-kept lawns reaching down to the river's edge.*
It	*was*	*one of the nicest houses in these parts.*
The Rat	*disembarked.*	
Toad	*had bought*	*a shining new canary yellow gipsy caravan with red wheels.*
Participant	**Process**	**Participant**
↘	↘	↘
noun group/ pronoun	verb group	noun group

- exploring illustrations and noun groups in picture books to identify how the noun groups have been represented by an illustrator [Year 2]

- creating richer, more specific descriptions through the use of noun groups (for example in narrative texts, 'Their very old Siamese cat'; in reports, 'Its extremely high mountain ranges' [Year 4]

---

32 These are sometimes called nominal groups or noun phrases.

The noun group is a valuable language resource as it can be extended in many ways to provide rich and detailed information about the person or thing engaged in the process. Unfortunately, some students don't take advantage of all the possibilities offered by the noun group, so it is worth spending some time on such features to improve students' writing. Noun groups are particularly important in text-types such as narratives (eg in setting the scene or describing a character) and information reports (eg in presenting information about a class of things). When students are reading, it is useful if they can see the noun group as 'a chunk of information' rather than a string of individual words, as in the following sentence:

I felt like throttling	***those two scruffy alley cats on the roof that were yowling all night.***
	NOUN GROUP

To show how the noun group expands, we can ask what type of information is being added:

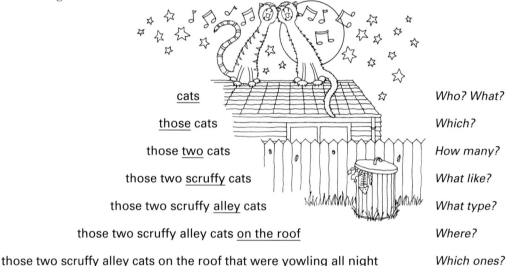

cats	Who? What?
those cats	Which?
those two cats	How many?
those two scruffy cats	What like?
those two scruffy alley cats	What type?
those two scruffy alley cats on the roof	Where?
those two scruffy alley cats on the roof that were yowling all night	Which ones?

■ using selected nouns as a basis for building extended noun groups that provide a clear description of an item [Year 2]

We can say that the underlined information is modifying the head noun.

those two scruffy alley	*cats*	***on the roof that were yowling all night***
pre-modifiers	noun	**post**-modifiers
NOUN GROUP		

In the following sections, we'll look at each of these resources for providing information.

Who? What? (Thing)

The head of the noun group is typically a person or thing. To identify the head word we ask 'who?' or 'what?'. We can use the term 'Thing' for this. The Thing typically takes the form of a noun or pronoun. The cats, for example, can be described as the 'Thing' that we are talking about. In this case the Thing is realised or expressed by the grammatical class of 'noun'. As before, it's always useful to start off with a probe question – 'who or what is the thing we are talking about?', drawing students' attention to the key word.

	Who or what?
	cats
MEANING	*Thing* ↘
FORM	noun

Certain nouns refer to things that are able to be counted (eg *ten apples, a couple of books, several nuns*). Some nouns, however, refer to things that are seen as an uncountable mass (eg *air, intelligence, research, information, water, happiness, respect, snow, advice, furniture, hair, homework, traffic, politics*). Uncountable nouns generally represent qualities, substances, and abstract notions. Some nouns can be both countable and uncountable (eg *ten cakes/some cake; Australian wines/a sip of wine*).

TROUBLESHOOTING

1 Students can experience problems when talking about amounts in relation to countable and uncountable nouns; for example, the difference between *'eat **less** butter'* (uncountable) and *'eat **fewer** chips'* (countable); or between *'there's not **much** traffic'* (uncountable) and *'there aren't **many** cars'* (countable).

2 Uncountable nouns can often cause difficulties for EAL students who might use them in the plural (eg 'We don't have a lot of informations').

To make a noun plural, we generally add **-s** to the end of the noun (eg *horses, storeys, spas*).

TROUBLESHOOTING

Some nouns form their plural in ways that can be confusing for some students:

- if a noun ends in **-x**, **-s**, **-ss**, **-sly -ch**, or **-z**, then we add **-es** (eg *boxes, buses, losses, brushes, branches, quizzes*)

- most nouns ending in **-o** add **-es** for the plural (eg *potatoes, heroes, mosquitoes*) but some (mainly abbreviated nouns) simply add -s (eg *photos, kilos, videos, radios, stereos*)

- when a noun ends in a consonant followed by **-y**, we form the plural with **-ies** (eg *ponies, stories*)

- certain nouns that end in **-f** or **-fe** form their plural with **-ves** (eg *halves, wives, knives*) though others will simply take an **-s** (eg *beliefs, chiefs, proofs, roofs*)

- some nouns from other languages have 'foreign' plurals (eg *phenomenon* ▶ *phenomena; criterion* ▶ *criteria; nucleus* ▶ *nuclei; referendum* ▶ *referenda; analysis* ▶ *analyses; vertebra* ▶ *vertebrae; formula* ▶ *formulae; appendix* ▶ *appendices*);

- some nouns change to a different form in the plural (eg *children, women, mice*)
- some nouns have the same form for both singular and plural (eg *deer, sheep, aircraft, fruit, species*)
- some nouns are always in the plural form (eg *scissors, trousers, underpants, pliers, glasses*). If we want to specify how many, we have to say, for example, 'three pairs of scissors'.

Information can be added both **before** the Thing and **after** the Thing,[33] providing such detail as:

- Which specific thing is being referred to?
- Who does it belong to?
- How many things are involved?
- What is the speaker's opinion about this thing?
- What attributes does it have? (eg size, shape, colour, size)
- How does it compare with other things?
- What class of things does it belong to?

	those two scruffy alley	cats	on the roof that were yowling all night.
I felt like throttling	pre-modifier	Thing	post-modifier
	NOUN GROUP		

Let's look at the different resources in the noun group – first those that come before the Thing (pre-modifier) and then those that come after (post-modifier). To do this, we'll be using functional terms to refer to the function or meaning. We can also use formal terms to refer to the grammatical form used to express these meanings.

Which one/s? (Pointers)

	Which?	Who or what?
I felt like throttling	those	cats
	Pointer	Thing

We use the everyday functional term Pointer[34] to refer to those words in the noun group that point to a specific person or thing: this one; that one; these ones; those ones; the one; his one; her one. These answer the question 'Which one/s in particular?'. Pointers can tell us whether the Thing is general (*a/an*) or specific (*the*), whether is it near (*this, these*) or far (*that, those*), and whether it is owned by anyone or anything (*my, John's, a friend's*).

---

[33] Technically, these are called Pre-modifiers and Post-modifiers.
[34] The technical term for Pointer is Deictic.

The function of Pointer can be expressed through many different grammatical forms. These cluster under the term 'determiner' and include articles, demonstratives and possessives.

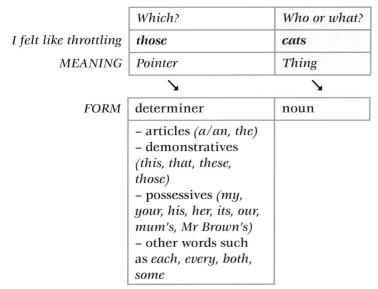

	Which?	Who or what?
I felt like throttling	**those**	**cats**
MEANING	Pointer	Thing

FORM	determiner	noun
	– articles *(a/an, the)* – demonstratives *(this, that, these, those)* – possessives *(my, your, his, her, its, our, mum's, Mr Brown's)* – other words such as *each, every, both, some*	

TROUBLESHOOTING

For native speakers of English, determiners pose no particular problems and it is hardly worth spending time on teaching these systematically, unless to clarify certain points. For many learners of English, however, some determiners can cause considerable difficulties and they might need quite a bit of practice with these.

Articles

The articles in English are used to give an indication about the degree to which a reference to something is general or specific. If it is a general reference, we use the **indefinite article** – 'a' or 'an' (eg *We saw **a** whale.*). If it is specific we use the **definite article** – 'the' (eg *The whale plunged into the water.*). Articles can be used to form links in a text.[35] When, for example, we have already introduced the thing we are talking about in general terms (eg *a whale*) and now want to refer back to it more specifically, we use the definite article (eg *the whale*). Often, however, we don't have to introduce the thing to our listener or reader because we can assume that they would realise what we meant from the context (eg ***The** rain had stopped now, and **the** sky was clearing.*).

The indefinite article is usually 'a', but it changes to 'an' in front of a word beginning with a vowel sound (eg ***an** elephant*) or a silent 'h' (eg ***an** hour*). In the plural, we might use no article (*Movies are expensive.*) or a word like 'some' (*Some movies are expensive.*).

The definite article has only one form: 'the'. It is used in front of both singular and plural nouns (eg ***the** boy/**the** boys*).

---

[35] See Chapter 5 for notes on the cohesive function of articles and other determiners.

TROUBLESHOOTING

Generally the use of the articles is relatively straightforward and should not cause problems for students. It is the sort of knowledge that we pick up from immersion in the language and use subconsciously. Students learning English as an additional language (EAL) or as a second language (ESL), however, particularly those more recently arrived, could have difficulties knowing when to use 'a/an', when to use 'the', and when not to use anything. Look, for example, at how in English we can refer to a general class of things (eg in an information report):

> **The** whale is a mammal. (definite article)

> **Whales** are mammals. (no article)

> **A** whale is a mammal. (indefinite article)

Many languages use articles in quite different ways from English (or don't use articles at all), so some EAL students will need assistance in this area.

Demonstratives

There are only four demonstratives in English:

	near	far
singular	this	that
plural	these	those

Demonstratives tell us which specific thing is being referred to in terms of its distance in space and time. Is it the one close by (eg **this** apple/**these** apples)? Or is it further away (eg **that** apple/**those** apples)?

> Do you want **this** newspaper or **that** one?

> **These** batteries don't work.

> **These** days it's hard to find work.

> Watch out for **that** step.

> How much are **those** sneakers?

> At **that** stage, it didn't seem important.

Sometimes demonstratives can be used when we want to be more specific or more emphatic:

> It was on **that** particular voyage that the Lusitania was torpedoed

> **That's** what I meant!

> **This** little piggy went to market,
>
> **This** little piggy stayed home,
>
> **This** little piggy had roast beef,
>
> **This** little piggy had none,
>
> And **this** little piggy went wee-wee-wee-wee all the way home.

Demonstratives help to establish 'point of view', locating the speaker in relation to other people or things in the environment.

Possessives

Possessives[36] typically tell us who owns something.[37] In the poem below, notice how possessives are used to highlight the notion of ownership. The cat's world is carefully divided into 'mine' and 'yours', but even then it distinguishes between the possessions that have been given to it and the one possession it chose for itself. This poem could be used as a stimulus for a discussion on the nature of possessions and ownership (including the ownership of pets) and how these might differ from culture to culture.

> **My** dish,
> **My** toys,
> **My** basket,
> **My** scratching post and **my** Ping-Pong ball;
> You provided them for me.
> This chair I selected for myself.
>
> I like it,
> It suits me.
> You have the sofa,
> The stuffed chair
> And the footstool.
>
> I don't go and sit on them do I?
> Then why cannot you leave me mine,
> And let us have no further argument?
>
> Paul Gallico

TROUBLESHOOTING

1 The possessives 'his' and 'her' can also be a problem for ESL students whose home language does not, for example, differentiate between masculine and feminine possessives.

2 Some students have problems forming the possessive. The following rules show how to make a noun possessive:

- To make a singular noun possessive, add **'s**:
  eg *a dog's life; Brooke's bag; the boy's leg*

- If the noun ends in **s**, you can simply put an apostrophe:
  eg *James' car* (though sometimes this is written as *James's car*)

- If the noun is plural, put an apostrophe after the **s**:
  eg *the birds' nests, the students' lunches*

- If the plural is an irregular one (and does not end in **s**) add **'s**:

- eg *the women's toilets; some children's hair*

---

[36] There is a variety of possessive forms. If students are interested in these forms, most standard reference grammars will contain greater detail.

[37] Though the meaning is not always related to ownership, eg He was working in his office; She looks after her health.

A good rule of thumb is: Add **'s** to any noun to make it possessive, but if it already ends in s, simply move the apostrophe so it is after the **s**.

Note that **it's** is the contraction of **it is** – not the possessive form (**its**):

> *It's* quiet. (It is quiet.)   The dog ate *its* dinner. (the dog's dinner)

This is a common misunderstanding. Students in each stage might need to be reminded of this difference. It can be explored, for example, when doing guided reading with a book such as *Caterpillar Diary*:

> This caterpillar has shed *its* skin. Now *it's* green and it has grown a lot bigger.
> ... Last night my moth came out of *its* cocoon. I know *it's* a moth because *its* feelers are shaped like feathers.

How many? (Quantifiers)

In answer to the question 'How many?' or 'How much?', we can refer to various types of Quantifiers:[38]

- exact numbers (*ten, 153, a million*)

- inexact numbers or amounts (*few (of), several, great deal (of), cup (of), most, many*)

- ordinal numbers (*first, third, next, final*)

	Which?	*How many?*	*Who or what?*
I felt like throttling	*those*	*two*	*cats.*
MEANING	*Pointer*	*Quantifier*	*Thing*

FORM	determiner	numeral	noun

With young children, we often use the term 'number words' before introducing the term 'Quantifier'.

> **Five** little rabbits sat under a tree,
>
> The **first** one said, "What can I see?"
>
> The **second** one said, "A man with a gun."
>
> The **third** one said, "Quick, let's run!"
>
> The **fourth** one said, "Let's hide in the shade!"
>
> The **fifth** one said, "I'm not afraid".
>
> "Bang!" went the gun and missed every one.
>
> *Understanding Mathematics 5: How many*, A. Davidson

Quantifiers are often found in maths problems and procedures.[39]

---

[38] Quantifiers are often included in the category of determiners.
[39] In formal written texts, numbers below 100 are generally written as words, but in mathematics and science word problems, the number symbols are used.

> Evan delivers packages in a building.
>
> He started on the **first** floor and went up **7** floors.
>
> He went down **3** floors and then up **16** floors.
>
> Then he was only **2** floors away from the top of the building.
>
> How many floors are in the building altogether?

Apart from these precise references to numbers, we can also have more vague references to quantities and amounts: *most of the boys; many babies; a few dollars; several reasons; too much cake.*

Sometimes it is important to be precise (eg in providing statistical evidence for an argument or in a maths problem). At other times, we might want to use more indefinite terms. These are often found in information reports (eg **Most** *herbivores* ...; *but a* **few** ...) and in expositions (**The great majority of** *scientists agree* ...).

Here are some inexact Quantifiers:[40]

> *a lot of; a little; another; a bag of; enough; all; a bit of; several; much; plenty of; numerous; various; more; a few; less; many.*

What's it like? (Describers)

	Which?	How many?	What like?	Who or what?
I felt like throttling	*those*	*two*	***scruffy***	*cats*
MEANING	*Pointer*	*Quantifier*	*Describer*	*Thing*
	↘	↘	↘	↘
FORM	determiner	numeral	adjective or *–ed* word or *–ing* word	noun

The function of describing (Describer)[41] is typically realised by the grammatical class of adjective.

> Understand that noun groups can be expanded using articles and adjectives [Year 2]

Describers can provide factual information (*the* **red** *box; a* **large** *car*) or a more personal opinion (*my* **sweet** *baby; a* **stupid** *remark*). Evaluative Describers tend to precede factual ones (*an* **exciting new** *idea*).

Factual Describers

Factual Describers describe something in an objective way. They describe the qualities that a thing possesses: its size; age; shape; colour; and other characteristics.

---

[40] Some of them can go in front of a determiner, in which case they are called 'pre-determiners', eg **some** *of the trees,* **all** *his dinner.*

[41] This is sometimes referred to by the technical term Epithet.

These Describers are found in most text types, but particularly in information reports, descriptions and procedures.

> *Blue heelers have a **thickset** body with **pricked** ears. They have a **smooth, mottled-blue** coat and a **red** or **black** face with a **dark, round** spot over each eye.*

While most Describers provide a description which is everyday and concrete, it is possible to find Describers that are more technical and/or abstract:

> **nutritious** *foods*
>
> *a* **contagious** *disease*
>
> **nitrogen-rich** *soil*
>
> *a* **practical** *solution.*

Apart from adjectives, the function of describing can also be expressed through **-ing** words derived from verbs (*the swinging rope; a dancing bear*) or **-ed** words derived from verbs (*a wasted opportunity; a peeled apple*). Note how these can function to 'condense' meaning – instead of saying:

> *he wasted the opportunity*

we can downgrade this clause to simply part of a noun group*:*

> *an opportunity **that was wasted***

or, in an even more compact form:

> *a **wasted** opportunity.*

Such compacting is typical of the written language of educational contexts over which learners need to develop control.

Similarly we can have compound adjectives that compact information. Instead of saying:

> *Next they met an emu and it had a long neck and it had long legs and it had sharp claws.*

we could say:

> *Next they met a **long-necked, long-legged, sharp-clawed** emu.*

A noun group can include any number of Describers, though too many tend to sound clumsy. Sometimes Describers are joined by 'and' or 'but' (*a **sad and lonely** child; a **cheap but effective** solution*).

Evaluative Describers

If we want to express our evaluation of something, we can use a Describer that indicates an opinion. While most other adjectives are used to build up a picture of the world, evaluative Describers have a more interpersonal function.[42] When we give our opinion, we are creating a situation where our listener or reader will

---

[42] See Chapter 4, Interacting with Others, for further discussion of how these more 'interpersonal' Describers express attitude.

probably react, either agreeing with our evaluation or taking issue with it. The opinion invites us not simply to observe but to interact.

This type of Describer is important in critical reading activities, where students need to identify how, for example, a newspaper article or magazine story or television documentary is influencing them to see things in a particular way. Evaluative Describers are generally not used in text types such as information reports and explanations.

In their own writing, students need to extend their repertoire of evaluative Describers so that they are able to express their opinions on things, people and situations in less clichéd, more subtle and convincing ways (eg in stories, recounts, biographies, and expositions). In extending their pool of Describers, students could use a thesaurus to look for synonyms. Synonyms for the word 'terrible', for example, would include:

abhorrent	appalling	atrocious	awful	beastly
desperate	dire	disastrous	disturbing	dreadful
fearful	frightful	ghastly	gruesome	harrowing
hateful	hideous	horrendous	horrid	horrifying
loathsome	monstrous	obnoxious	odious	offensive
petrifying	repulsive	revolting	shocking	vile

Students could also find antonyms for *'terrible'*:

| alluring | appealing | delightful | desirable | enjoyable |
| likeable | lovable | pleasant | sweet | wonderful |

A common activity is to ask students to arrange evaluative Describers along a continuum, eg:

deadly dull → boring → so so → mildly interesting → fascinating

It is possible, particularly in more literary texts, to place the Describers after the Thing:

Emma Woodhouse,	*handsome, clever, and rich …*
Thing	**Describers**

It was	*a lovely morning,*	*cool and fresh.*
	Thing	**Describers**

Adjusting the degree

Most Describers can be modified in terms of the degree of intensity:[43]

> an **extremely expressive** grimace
>
> a **very delicate** affair
>
> a **somewhat odd** story

---

[43] See also Chapter 4, Interacting with Others, p.125

> a **slightly different** *way*
> a **rather** *long movie*
> a **really convincing** *argument*
> a **very strong** *smell*
> some **incredibly cheap** *bargains*
> that **dark blue** *shirt.*

We can also intensify a description by repeating the Describer:

> 'Oh, you **wicked wicked** little thing!' cried Alice.
>
> It was a **big big** surprise.

Making comparisons

We can use Describers to compare one thing with another. Such Describers are often referred to as comparatives (eg *smarter*) and superlatives (eg *the smartest*).

To make a comparative or superlative, you add **-er** or **-est** to the adjective:

> *long*   →   *longer/longest*
> *sad*   →   *sadder/saddest*

> If Rabbit
>
> Was **bigger**
>
> And **fatter**
>
> And **stronger**,
>
> Or **bigger**
>
> **Than Tigger**,
>
> If Tigger was **smaller**,
>
> Then Tigger's bad habit
>
> Of bouncing at Rabbit
>
> Would matter no longer,
>
> If Rabbit
>
> Was **taller**.
>
> A.A. Milne

TROUBLESHOOTING

Note that when **-er** and **-est** are added to some endings, there is a spelling change (eg a final single consonant following a single vowel is doubled (*slimmer*) before adding the comparative endings).

If the adjective has two syllables or more, then the words *more* and *most* are used with the adjective rather than adding the endings *-er* and *-est*:

> *complicated* ▶ *more complicated/most complicated*

those two scruffy alley cats	*that were yowling all night*
the spectacled gentleman	*who sat at the head of the table*
a little dark-eyed man	*whom his mates called Smoke*
the place	*where I grew up*
	embedded clause

NOUN GROUP

This is the Farmer **that** sowed the corn,

That fed the cock **that** crowed in the morn,

That waked the priest all shaven and shorn,

That married the man all tattered and torn,

That kissed the maiden all forlorn,

That milked the cow with the crumpled horn,

That tossed the dog,

That worried the cat,

That killed the rat,

That ate the malt,

That lay in the house that Jack built.

The relative pronouns **who** and **whom** refer to persons. **Who** is the Subject and **whom** is the Object.[48]

> *The person **who** was just speaking ...* (Subject of the verb 'was speaking')
>
> *The person **whom** I drove to the station ...* (Object of the verb 'drove')
>
> *The person <u>to</u> **whom** he gave the briefcase ...* (Object of the preposition 'to')

These days the **whom** form is not commonly used, particularly in spoken language (eg '*The person* [who] *I drove to the station*'; *The person* [who] *he gave the briefcase to*').

The relative pronoun **that** can be used with either people or things.

> *The person **that** I want to meet ...*
>
> *The train **that** was late ...*

The relative pronoun **which** is generally only used with things.

> *The movie **which** was released last week ...*
>
> *The town <u>to</u> **which** I was travelling ...*

---

[48] See below for explanation of Subject and Object.

The relative pronoun **whose** (the possessive form) can be used with people or things:

> People **whose** opinion I respect ...

> A country **whose** population is growing ...

Sometimes, however, there is no relative pronoun and not even a full verb group:[49]

those two scruffy alley cats	*~~that were~~ **yowling** all night*
the tall man	*~~who was~~ **standing** in the doorway*
a tiny little room	*~~that was~~ **filled** with vases of flowers*
so many things	*~~that need~~ **to be done***
	embedded clause

NOUN GROUP

TROUBLESHOOTING

This more complex use of language is regarded as more mature and concise and should be encouraged in older students' writing. Students often write a series of short, choppy sentences rather than compacting the information by using a Qualifier:

> *There was a girl. She was in my class. Her name was Kim. She lived with her grandmother.*

There was	a girl	in my class	named Kim	who lived with her grandmother.
		Qualifier (prep phrase)	Qualifier (embedded clause)	Qualifier (embedded clause)

NOUN GROUP

Some students may have trouble comprehending texts that contain such structures. In this case, it is often useful to demonstrate how to 'unpack' the noun group:

> *Musical instruments **that are played by hitting or shaking** belong to the percussion group.*
> *Some instruments are played by hitting (eg a drum).*
> *Some instruments are played by shaking (eg a tambourine).*
> *These instruments belong to the percussion group.*

Understand the use of vocabulary to express greater precision of meaning [Year 5]

In assessing students' literacy, we could consider how well our students are exploiting the possibilities offered by the noun group. Are they sticking to simple, 'safe' noun

---

[49] These are called 'non-finite' clauses. See p. 98

groups? Or are they perhaps using short, simple groups for a particular effect? Are they experimenting with longer groups containing a variety of resources, such as building up the description in an information report? Are they able to comprehend more complex noun groups in their reading? Are their reading materials providing them with good, challenging models of complex noun groups? In which types of text are you more likely to find lengthy noun groups? Are they able to perceive a cluster of words as a noun group as opposed to a string of single items?

Looking at form: Pronouns

There are many different types of pronouns. Here we will only look in any detail at a couple: personal pronouns and possessive pronouns.[50]

In addition to noun groups, Participants can also be realised by personal pronouns and by possessive pronouns:

	They	*stopped short suddenly.*
MEANING	Participant ↘	
FORM	personal pronoun	

	Mine	*is the pink one.*
MEANING	Participant ↘	
FORM	possessive pronoun	

Personal pronouns

Personal pronouns are used to refer to the person who is speaking (the 'first' person), the person being spoken to (the 'second' person), or the person/thing being spoken about (the 'third' person). They can refer to one person or thing (singular) or more than one (plural). We can divide personal pronouns into those that act as Subject of the verb and those that act as Object of the verb:

	SINGULAR		PLURAL	
	Subject	**Object**	**Subject**	**Object**
1st person *(speaking)*	I	me	we	us
2nd person *(spoken to)*	you	you	you	you
3rd person *(spoken of)*	he she it	him her it	they	them

---

[50] See also relative pronouns on p.58

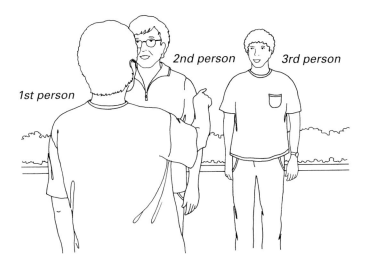

Personal pronouns can be:

- the Subject of the verb (typically coming before the verb)

SUBJECT OF VERB	
I	*heard the news yesterday.*
We	*wanted to come with you.*
You	*should have told Mrs Peters.*
He	*was in the bathroom.*
She	*spoke very slowly.*
It	*refused to budge.*
They	*opened it carefully.*

- or the Object of the verb (typically following the verb)

	OBJECT OF VERB	
Susan told	*me*	*the whole story.*
That path takes	*us*	*to the north.*
Cigarettes will kill	*you.*	
The guards dragged	*him*	*from the building.*
They transferred	*her*	*to intensive care.*
Then place	*it*	*in the cold water.*
You can see	*them*	*through the microscope.*

- or the Object of a preposition.

	OBJECT OF PREPOSITION	
She sat	*near **me***	*on the bus.*
He didn't even wait	*for **us.***	
I saw him give it	*to **you***	*last night.*
It all depends	*on **him.***	
He threw his arms	*around **her.***	
They left	*without **it.***	
The smoke swirled	*about **them.***	

TROUBLESHOOTING

In informal spoken dialects, Object pronouns are often used instead of Subject pronouns:

✗ ***Him and me** are going to the park.* (✔ *He and I are going to the park.*)

While this is common in casual, familiar contexts, it is generally not used in written academic contexts.

Similarly, using the Subject pronoun instead of the Object pronoun is found in spoken language, particularly when trying to sound 'formal', even though technically it is not accurate:

✗ *She gave it to John and I.* (✔ *She gave it to John and me.*)

This can be detected by removing the first noun – eg *She gave it to I –* which sounds odd.

Possessive pronouns

Possessive pronouns can also function as a Participant:

*That is **my towel**.* → *That is **mine**.*

***Your towel** is on the floor.* → ***Yours** is on the floor.*

In the above cases, 'mine' and 'yours' are Participants expressed by possessive pronouns.

	singular	plural
1st person[51]	mine	ours
2nd person	yours	yours
3rd person	his/hers	theirs

*That's not her umbrella, it's **mine** [my umbrella]!*

*You've got your dinner, now we want **ours** [our dinner].*

*This is Michael's T-shirt. **Hers** [her T-shirt] is in the washing machine.*

---

[51] First person refers to the speaker, second person to who is being spoken to, and third person who/what is being spoken about.

These are similar in meaning to the possessive determiners that we met earlier in the noun group (eg *it's **my** umbrella*), but in the case of possessive pronouns, they are not part of the noun group – they replace the noun group (eg *it's **mine***).

Looking at form: The adjective group

Although we generally think of Participants as 'persons' or 'things', sometimes a Participant can take the form of an adjective or adjective group. This is typically found in clauses with relating verbs, where something is being described. In a grammatical sense, the adjective group is 'participating' in the description.[52]

Participant (eg 'thing being described')	Relating verb	Participant (eg 'description') ↘ adjective group
She	*was*	*too **busy** to listen.*
The shop owner	*became*	***enraged.***
The children	*seemed*	*somewhat **subdued.***

In the sentences above, the relating verb is linking someone or something to its description (or 'attribute'). The description takes the form of an adjective group.

Sometimes there may simply be a single adjective:

Alice	*was*	***frightened.***

> Understand how noun and adjective groups can be expanded in a variety of ways to provide a fuller description of the person, thing or idea [Year 5]

But, as with the noun group, more information can be added before the head adjective (ie a premodifier).

Alice	*was*	*very **frightened.***

Information can also be added after the head adjective (ie a postmodifier):

Alice	*was*	***frightened** of the Rabbit.*

Or, information can be added both before and after the head adjective:

Alice	*was*	*so **frightened** that she couldn't speak.*
Alice	*was*	*the most **frightened** she had ever been.*
Alice	*was*	*more **frightened** than before.*

We can represent the structure of the adjective group as follows:

---

[52] This is sometimes referred to as a Complement.

ADJECTIVE GROUP		
so	frightened	that she couldn't speak.
the most	frightened	she had ever been.
more	frightened	than before.
premodifier	**adjective**	**postmodifier**

Modifiers before the head adjective are usually intensifiers:[53]

really	frightened
intensifier	

Modifiers following the head adjective can be either a prepositional phrase or an embedded clause:

frightened	of the Rabbit
	prepositional phrase

frightened	to go outside
	embedded clause

TROUBLESHOOTING

In descriptive writing, students often don't take full advantage of the adjective group. It is worth pointing out rich adjective groups during shared reading and adding them to wall charts as they are encountered. In *Alice in Wonderland*, for example, adjective groups abound:

'I'm quite *tired* of being such a tiny little thing!'

It was very *uncomfortable*.

'It was much *pleasanter* at home.'

'Shall I NEVER get any *older* than I am now'

'I'm a deal too *flustered* to tell you.'

She was *delighted* to find that she began shrinking directly.

She was *small* enough to get through the door.

She was terribly *frightened* at the thought that it might be hungry.

Looking at form: Clause as Participant

Just as we might not think of an adjective group as a Participant in the more everyday sense, so we might not consider a clause as a potential Participant. But again, in a grammatical sense, a clause can function as a Participant. While we might not want to spend time on this with students, it is handy to know in case questions are raised. Here are a few examples without going into detail:

---

[53] Or in formal terms, these are adverbs modifying an adjective.

Participant	Relating verb	Participant ↘ clause
Her main aim	was	[[to save enough money for her holiday]].
Their favourite recreation	is	[[driving down the coast]].
The time [[she liked best]]	was	[[when the cockatoos shrieked at dawn]].
The reason [[they left]]	was	[[because the play was boring]].[54]

Participant ↘ clause	Relating verb	Participant
[[That they were late]]	was not	a problem.
[[Whizzpopping]]	is	a sign of happiness.

When clauses serve the function of Participant, we say they are 'embedded',[55] as they are part of a larger clause and don't have the status of a separate clause themselves. The larger clause is often one that contains a relating verb (as above), though this is not necessarily the case:

[[Worrying about her weight]]	didn't help	the situation.
[[Learning to be a reader]]	gives	a terrific advantage.
[[That she didn't say hello]]	upset	me.

Recognise and understand that embedded clauses are a common feature of sentence structures and contribute additional information to a sentence [Year 7]

Clauses functioning as Participants[56] are not uncommon, particularly in written language:

> I was already beginning to realise that the only way to conduct oneself in a situation where bombs rained down and bullets whizzed past, was **[[to accept the dangers and all the consequences as calmly as possible]]. [[Fretting and sweating about it all]]** was not going to help.
>
> *Going Solo*, R. Dahl

We can now summarise the various grammatical forms that can be used to realise the meaning of 'Participant':

---

[54] Notice that embedded clauses (that is clauses that are part of another clause or part of a noun group) can be indicated by using double square brackets.

[55] Embedded clauses are also found in the noun group: the time [[she liked best]].

[56] Traditionally, some types of 'clauses as Participants' have been referred to as gerunds, verbal nouns or noun clauses.

MEANING	Who or what is involved in the process? (Participants)	

↘

FORM	noun group	Alice had put on **one of the Rabbit's little white kid gloves.**
	pronoun	**She** dropped **it** hastily.
	adjective group	Alice was **very glad** [[to find herself still in existence]].
	embedded clause	Her first idea was [[that she had somehow fallen into the sea]].

Of these, it is perhaps the noun group that provides the richest and most flexible resource for fleshing out the Participants in an activity. Students need to know when to use short, snappy noun groups and when to pack them with information. They need to investigate how good writers construct effective noun groups to make their texts more precise, more compact or more vivid.

What are the details surrounding the activity?

We've seen how a clause represents experience by depicting various kinds of processes and the participants in those processes. But that doesn't give us enough information. We need to know more about the process – when is it happening? Where? Why? How? With whom? We refer to these as the Circumstances surrounding the activity.

Where?	Who/what is taking part?	What's happening?	How?
High in the treetop	the cat	was smiling	**mysteriously.**
Circumstance			Circumstance
CLAUSE			

While students will comprehend and use many of the more straightforward Circumstances, an explicit knowledge of all the options available to them will help to extend their language repertoire and their ability to construct more expressive and complex meanings.

Looking at meaning: Different kinds of Circumstances

The Circumstances tell us about such matters as time, place, manner, accompaniment, matter, cause, contingency, role, and angle. These details are obviously important in enabling students to comprehend and express aspects of their experience. Let's look at some examples of these.

Understand how ideas can be expanded and sharpened through careful choice of a range of adverbials [Year 6]

TIME

When? **(Point in time)**	*I'll see you **at eight o'clock**.* *He's got an appointment **in the morning**.* *She sprained her ankle **yesterday**.* *We're going over there **now**.*
How long? **(Duration in time)**	*I haven't seen him **for ages**.* *That film lasted **forever**.* ***During this period** he was unemployed.*
'How many times?' **(Frequency)**	*We play tennis **every Saturday**.* *They **regularly** visit his mother.* ***On weekdays** she catches the bus.* *We **often** see him at the pub.*

PLACE

Where? **(Point in space)**	*I'll see you **there**.* *Place the eggs **in the bowl**.* *He snuggled **under the warm blankets**.*
Where to/from? **(Direction)**	*He was walking **backwards**.* *They drove **towards the village**.*
How far? (Distance)	*We walked **for miles**.*

MANNER

How? (Quality)	***Slowly**, she made her way through the crowd.* *The singers performed **well**.*
By what means? (Means)	*Beat the mixture **with a fork**.* *They travelled **by train**.*
What like? (Comparison)	*She laughed **like a hyena**.* ***Unlike her mother**, she enjoyed reading.*
How much? (Degree)	***To a large extent** they only had themselves to blame.* *She always pays **too much**.* *She loved him **deeply**.*

ACCOMPANIMENT

Who/what with? **(In the company of)**	*She went to the dentist **alone**.* ***Together** they fought for justice.* *He left **with Susan**.*
And who/what else? **(In addition)**	*There was blancmange **as well as jelly**.* ***Besides her best friend**, no-one knew her secret.* *The children cleaned up **instead of their mother**.*

MATTER

What about? (Topic)	***Regarding your question**, can you put it in writing?* *They talked all night **about the situation**.*

CAUSE	
Why? (Reason)	**Due to poor visibility**, the flight will be cancelled. **As a result of her illness**, she was unable to continue. They invited her **out of pity**.
Why? What for? (Purpose)	He was making lasagne **for dinner**. She went to the party **in the hope of seeing him**.
Who for? (Behalf)	I wanted to thank you **on our behalf**. Mick laid the table **for his mother**.
CONTINGENCY	
What if ...? (Condition)	**In case of cancellation**, tickets will be refunded. **In the event of a draw**, there will be a penalty shootout.
Although ...? (Concession)	Beached whale dies, **despite rescue attempts**. They let him play **in spite of their misgivings**.
ROLE	
What as? (Guise)	**As an expert in the field**, she was often asked for her opinion. **In his role as president**, he chaired the meeting.
ANGLE	
According to whom?' (Source)	**In the words of Martin Luther King Jr.**, a right delayed is a right denied. **According to you**, I'm difficult.
In whose view? (Viewpoint)	**In my opinion**, she could do much better. **From the consumer's perspective**, it's a legitimate gripe.

- investigating in texts how adverbial phrases and clauses can add significance to an action, for example 'more desperately', 'he rose quietly and gingerly moved' [Year 4]

Certain text types (eg recounts, stories) will focus on Circumstances that tell us when something happened, where it happened and in what manner. Text types such as procedures will rely on precise Circumstances to provide such information as: How long? In which way? By what means? How frequently? Explanations and expositions might include Circumstances of cause and reason.

TROUBLESHOOTING

While most students don't have problems with the more common Circumstances, it is important that they are able to use and comprehend an increasing range of more varied and complex Circumstances (eg fine distinctions of time and place; meanings relating to cause, contingency, angle, role, etc).

Looking at form: The grammar of Circumstances

We have seen that Circumstances provide all sorts of information about the activity. In terms of form, Circumstances are typically realised by two main grammatical categories: adverbs/adverb groups and prepositional phrases, though occasionally they might take the form of other categories such as the noun group.

MEANING	providing details about an activity (Circumstances)	
	↘	
FORM	adverbs	She dropped it **hastily**.
	adverb groups	'Found it,' the Mouse replied **rather crossly**.
	prepositional phrases	The little golden key was lying **on the glass table**.
	noun groups	**Some winter day**, I will tell you how the Dodo managed it.

Adverbs, adverb groups, prepositional phrases and other ways of representing Circumstances are often grouped together under the term 'adverbials'.

> Understand how adverbials (adverbs and prepositional phrases) work in different ways to provide circumstantial details about an activity [Year 4]

Adverbs as Circumstances

Adverbs have a number of functions. They can, for example, indicate degree[57] (**very** happy, **almost** ready), or make links in texts[58] (**subsequently**), or create comparisons[59] (**more** intelligent). Here however we are concerned with how they function to represent the Circumstances surrounding an activity.

> I never go **there**.
>
> They **quickly** left the room.
>
> She arrived **early**.

Adverbs typically consist of a single word.[60] They are often constructed by adding **-ly** to an adjective (stupid ▶ stupid**ly**; careful ▶ careful**ly**), though many are not (eg yesterday, there, upstairs, early).

---

[57] See section in Interacting with Others, p.126
[58] See section in Creating Cohesive Texts p.153
[59] See Making Comparisons in this chapter, p.52
[60] Even though adverbs might consist of a single word, they are often included in the grammatical class of 'adverb group'.

TROUBLESHOOTING

Note that when the adjective ends in *-y*, you need to change the '*y*' to '*i*' before adding *-ly*: happy → happily

angry → angrily

Adverb groups as Circumstances

Just as nouns can be the head of a noun group, and adjectives can be the head of an adjective group, so adverbs can be the head of an adverb group. We can expand around the adverb by adding detail both before the adverb (premodifiers) and after the adverb (postmodifiers).

ADVERB GROUP		
extremely	quickly	
as	quickly	as possible
more	quickly	than before
so	quickly	that he fell over
too	quickly	to notice
premodifier	**adverb**	**postmodifier**

As with the adjective group, the modifiers before the head adverb generally indicate degree (*extremely, too*) and comparison (*more*) while the modifiers following the head adverb can take the form of a prepositional phrase (*than before*) or an embedded clause (*that he fell over, to notice*).

Prepositional phrases as Circumstances

Circumstances can also take the form of a prepositional phrase[61] – that is, a preposition followed by a noun group.[62]

near *the house*

at *dawn*

in *a deep voice*

with *her mother*

Note that prepositional phrases can do different jobs. They can function both as Qualifiers and as Circumstances (in a clause). When they function as a Qualifier in the noun group, they provide more information about the Thing:

The high note	*at the start*	*was a bit flat.*
Thing	Qualifier	
NOUN GROUP		

---

[61] When prepositional phrases are used to provide information about an activity, they are often called adverbial phrases.
[62] See Prepositional Phrase as Qualifier in this chapter, p.54.

When they function as a Circumstance, however, they are providing detail about the Process.

He faltered	at the start.
Process	**Circumstance**

In the first example, the prepositional phrase *at the start* is giving more information about a Thing (*the high* **note**). It is part of the noun group and functioning as a Qualifier. In the second example, the same prepositional phrase – *at the start* – is providing detail about a Process (*faltered*) – that is, it answers the question 'When did he falter?'. In this case it is a Circumstance. Note that prepositional phrases functioning as Circumstances can often move around the clause, providing the writer with more options to change the focus when structuring sentences.

He faltered	at the start.
Process	**Circumstance**

At the start,	he faltered.
Circumstance	**Process**

Whereas prepositional phrases functioning as Qualifiers are embedded in the noun group and can't move around. Here are some more examples:

Prepositional phrase as **Circumstance** (providing detail about the Process)		Prepositional phrase as **Qualifier** (providing detail about the Thing)	
Across the field *She ran*	*she ran.* *across the field.*	*the view*	*across the field*
During summer *They sweltered*	*they sweltered.* *during summer.*	*the heat*	*during summer*
By car *The trip takes an hour*	*the trip takes an hour.* *by car.*	*the trip*	*by car*
CLAUSE		*NOUN GROUP*	

Noun groups as Circumstances

Occasionally, Circumstances can take the form of a noun group:

> *He went **next door**.*

> *They played **all day**.*

> *They left **two years ago**.*

■ knowing that adverbials can provide important details about an action (for example 'At nine o'clock the buzzer rang loudly throughout the school.') [Year 6]

Circumstances in procedures, Circumstances of manner when building up a character in a story)?

■ Are they readily using a variety of Circumstances (eg place, time, manner, cause and accompaniment) in the form of both adverbs/adverb groups and prepositional phrases?

Older learners

Older learners are using language in quite sophisticated ways to represent what's going on in their world and in academic contexts. By now they should have developed a substantial metalanguage to discuss the texts they are reading and writing. They might reflect, for example, on the different types of clauses in a text and how these contribute to the meaning of the text: Who is doing the action?; Who is being affected by the action?; Who is the initiator?; Who is playing a more passive role?; Who does all the talking?; Why?; What sorts of things are being said?; Why is the writer telling us about the thoughts/feelings of a particular character?; What does this tell us about the character?

Teachers can ask questions such as the following to ascertain whether students are developing the language resources to express the kinds of meanings needed to succeed in secondary schooling.

■ In their reading, can they comprehend the clause as a meaningful unit and recognise the main components of the clause as significant 'chunks'?

■ Can they manipulate clause patterns when necessary in order to achieve particular effects (eg placing Describers after the noun: *I found a dimpled spider, fat and white*; omitting the verb: *Slowly. Very slowly.*)?

Processes

■ Are they understanding and employing a wide repertoire of different types of verbs, selecting those verbs that are most appropriate to express fine distinctions and detail (eg *grumbled, growled* or *thundered* instead of *said*).

■ In factual texts are they comprehending and using more technical verbs (eg *expand, contract, repel, magnetise*)?

■ In literary texts are they appreciating and attempting to use verbs that best develop the character, mood, action sequences or image?

■ Can they identify verb groups (including multi-word groups) in the texts they are reading?

■ Are they comprehending and constructing detailed verb groups that include more sophisticated use of tense and modality?

■ Can they recognise the function of different parts of the verb group, including a range of auxiliary verbs and modals?

■ Does their writing sounds immature/spoken because of overuse of phrasal verbs (*go back* vs. *return*) and 'empty' verbs (eg *have a look* vs. *observe*)?

Participants

■ Are they able to reflect on and discuss the noun groups in texts they are reading and writing and how well they serve their purpose in terms of representing particular ideas (eg literary, technical or abstract)?

■ Can they explain the function of different elements in the noun group (eg Classifier: to tell 'what type'; Qualifier: to specify 'which one')?

■ Are they employing a wide variety of noun groups to refer to the people, objects, places and concepts, expressing ideas involving fine distinctions and detail?

■ In literary texts are they appreciating and attempting to use noun groups that best capture the character, mood, setting, and so on?

■ Are they comprehending and constructing detailed noun groups that include various types of Qualifiers (prepositional phrases and embedded clauses): eg *Jonathan Kozol's Amazing Grace is a **book** [about the trials and tribulations [of everyday life] [for a group of children [[who live in the poorest congressional district [of the United States], the South Bronx]]]*.)?

■ Are they using extended adjective groups in their writing (*He was somewhat **peeved**; She grows particularly **hostile** towards Darcy.*)?

Circumstances

■ Are they using extended adverb groups (*What came next happened so fast [[no one saw how it happened]]*)?

■ Are they able to reflect on and employ the less common types of Circumstances in texts they are reading and writing and how they function to tell us more about an experience (eg For how long?; How frequently?; By what means?; What like?; What about?; For what reason?; To what end?; In spite of what?; In what role?; According to whom?)?

■ Are they using Circumstances that express fine distinctions and detail (eg *occasionally*; *from time to time*; or *intermittently* instead of simply *sometimes*)?

■ In factual texts are they comprehending and using more precise Circumstances (eg *in the winter of 1942; due to global warming; for two decades*)?

■ In literary texts are they appreciating and attempting to use Circumstances that best develop the character, mood or action sequences (eg *she murmured **lazily**; in the icy depths of winter*)?

■ Can they differentiate between prepositional phrases used as Circumstances (***In the mirror**, he could see ...*) and prepositional phrases used as Qualifiers (The face ***in the mirror*** was grimacing ...)?

Representing experience: Analysed text

The following text has been analysed to provide examples of the various resources involved in representing our experience of the world. This is not to suggest that students should be asked to analyse a text in this way.

- Embedded clauses are indicated by double square brackets [[...]].

- Embedded phrases are indicated by single square brackets [...].

- 'Joining words' haven't been analysed. (See next chapter.)

- Each element is analysed first in terms of its function (eg Participant) and then in terms of the particular grammatical form that is being used to express the function (eg noun group).

- The term 'Process' has been used to refer to the function (eg 'Process: saying' rather than 'saying verb').

As	she	said	these words
	Participant: sayer ↘	Process: saying ↘	Participant: 'what was said' ↘
	pronoun	verb	noun group

her foot	slipped,
Participant: 'do-er' ↘	Process: action ↘
noun group	verb

and	in another moment,	she	was	up to her chin	in salt water.
	Circumstance: time ↘	Participant: 'thing described' ↘	Process: relating ↘	Participant: 'description' ↘	Circumstance: place ↘
	prepositional phrase	pronoun	verb	prepositional phrase	prepositional phrase

Her first idea	was	[[that she had somehow fallen into the sea,]]
Participant: 'thing being identified' ↘	Process: relating ↘	Participant: 'identifier' ↘
noun group	verb	embedded clause

'and in that case	I		can go back	by railway,'
	Participant: 'do-er' ↘		Process: action ↘	Circumstance: means ↘
	pronoun		verb group	prepositional phrase

she	said	to herself.
Participant: sayer ↘	Process: saying ↘	Participant: receiver[62] ↘
pronoun	verb	prepositional phrase

(Alice	had gone	to the seaside	once,
Participant: 'do-er' ↘	Process: action ↘	Circumstance: place ↘	Circumstance: time ↘
noun	verb group	prepositional phrase	adverb

and	had concluded
	Process: sensing ('thinking') ↘
	verb group

that	every place [[you go to]] [on the English coast]	you	see
	Circumstance: place ↘	Participant: senser ↘	Process: sensing ('perceiving') ↘
	noun group	pronoun	verb

a number of bathing machines [in the sea],
Participant: 'what is sensed' ↘
noun group

---

[63] 'Receiver' hasn't been dealt with previously – it refers to the person or thing being spoken to.

some children [[digging in the sand with wooden spades]],		
Participant: 'what is sensed' ↘		
noun group		

then	a row of lodging houses,	
	Participant: 'what is sensed' ↘	
	noun group	

and	behind them	a railway station.)
	Circumstance: place ↘	Participant: 'what is sensed' ↘
	prepositional phrase	noun group

However,	she	soon	made out
	Participant: senser	Circumstance: time	Process: sensing ('thinking')
	pronoun	adverb	verb group

that	she	was	in the pool of tears [[which she had wept // when she was nine feet high]].
	Participant: 'described' ↘	Process: relating ↘	Circumstance: 'description of place' ↘
	pronoun	verb	prepositional phrase

'I	wish
Participant: senser ↘	Process: sensing ('desiring') ↘
pronoun	verb

I	hadn't cried	so much!'
Participant: 'do-er' ↘	Process: action ↘	Circumstance: degree ('how much?') ↘
pronoun	verb group	adverb group

said	Alice,
Process: saying ↘	Participant: sayer ↘
verb	noun

as	she	swam about,
	Participant: 'do-er' ↘	Process: action ↘
	pronoun	verb group

trying to find	her way out.
Process: action ↘	Participant: 'done-to' ↘
verb group	noun group

'I	shall be punished	for it	now,
Participant: 'done-to' ↘	Process: action ↘	Circumstance: reason ↘	Circumstance: time ↘
pronoun	verb group	prepositional phrase	adverb

I	suppose,
Participant: senser ↘	Process: sensing ('thinking') ↘
pronoun	verb

by	being drowned	in my own tears!
	Process: action ↘	Circumstance: place ↘
	verb group	prepositional phrase

That	WILL be	a queer thing!
Participant: 'thing described' ↘	Process: relating ↘	Participant: 'description' ↘
pronoun	verb group	noun group

However,	everything	is	queer	to-day.'
	Participant: 'thing described' ↘	Process: relating ↘	Participant: 'description' ↘	Circumstance: time ↘
	pronoun	verb	adjective	adverb

Just then	she	heard	[[something splashing about in the pool]]	a little way off,
	Participant: senser ↘	Process: sensing ('perceiving') ↘	Participant: 'what is sensed' ↘	Circumstance: place ↘
	pronoun	verb	embedded clause	noun group

and	she	swam	nearer
	Participant: 'do-er' ↘	Process: action ↘	Circumstance: place ↘
	pronoun	verb	adverb

to make out	[[what it was]]:
Process: sensing ('thinking') ↘	Participant: 'what is sensed' ↘
verb group	embedded clause

at first	she	thought
	Participant: senser ↘	Process: sensing ('thinking') ↘
	pronoun	verb

it	must be	a walrus or hippopotamus,
Participant: 'thing being identified' ↘	Process: relating ↘	Participant: 'identifier' ↘
pronoun	verb group	noun group

but then	*she*	*remembered*	*[[how small she was]]*	*now,*
	Participant: 'senser' ↘	Process: sensing ('thinking') ↘	Participant: 'what was sensed' ↘	Circumstance: time ↘
	pronoun	verb	embedded clause	adverb

and	*she*	*soon*	*made out*
	Participant: senser ↘	Circumstance: time ↘	Process: sensing ('thinking') ↘
	pronoun	adverb	verb group

that	*it*	*was*	*only a mouse [[that had slipped in like herself]].*
	Participant: 'thing being defined' ↘	Process: relating ↘	Participant: 'definition' identifier ↘
	pronoun	verb	noun group

Alice in Wonderland (amended excerpt), Lewis Carroll

3 Connecting ideas

Looking at meaning: Making connections

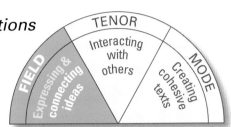

We have seen how clauses can function to represent various aspects of our experience: what is done; what is said; what is thought, felt or perceived, and what simply 'is'.

We can also construct relationships between these aspects of experience.

> Analyse and evaluate the effectiveness of a wide range of clause and sentence structures as authors design and craft texts [Year 10]

We can simply add two clauses together: *She opened her eyes **and** looked about her*.
Or we could provide alternatives: *To be **or** not to be.*
Or make a contrast: *I've got all my worldly goods in it, **but** it isn't heavy.*
Or we could speculate about 'What if?': *Which would you rather be **if** you had the choice – divinely beautiful or dazzlingly clever or angelically good?*
Or indicate cause and effect: *And people laugh at me **because** I use big words.*
Or show relationships of time: ***When** he reached Bright River, there was no sign of any train.*

It is through such connections that we are able to reason about our experience – to construct logical relationships. If learners are to be able to reason in increasingly sophisticated ways, they will need to expand their linguistic resources for connecting ideas.

> Investigate how clauses can be combined in a variety of ways to elaborate, extend or explain ideas [Year 6]

Structuring coherent sentences

A major skill that students need to develop is how to create well-structured sentences. Student texts often sound awkward because of the overuse of simple, single-clause sentences or because of the use of long, rambling, incoherent sentences.

Simple sentences are quite appropriate (and indeed functional) if used strategically. In text types such as newspaper stories, for example, they are typically short, uncluttered and 'to the point'. They are also effective when used at particular stages in a story – to disrupt the rhythm, to introduce a staccato effect or to make a significant point.

Longer sentences are appropriate, on the other hand, when there are a number of closely related ideas that need to be brought together. These sentences generally require careful crafting, however, and students need to be aware of the various ways in which information can be presented and clauses can be combined.

Look at the following text by a Year 1 student that uses a sequence of short sentences:

> *There was a giraffe. Her name was Gigi. She was grumpy. She was also old. And she had a long neck.*

This information could have been combined into a single clause by packaging much of the information in these sentences into one noun group:

> *Gigi was **a grumpy, old giraffe with a long neck**.*

Other sentences, especially in recounts and stories, often end up as a long string of clauses, resembling spoken language:

> *One day I was playing with my friends and I saw a ghost and it was flying towards me so I ran as fast as I could but then it disappeared then it appeared again so I ran for home then the ghost went through the wall then I went to my bedroom but the ghost went through my bedroom door then I woke up and it was all a dream.*

Apart from working on the development of this story, the student needs help with combining clauses into distinct sentences, eg:

> *One day, when I was playing with my friends, I saw a ghost flying towards me. I ran as fast as I could but then it disappeared. (Suddenly) it appeared again so I ran for home. But the ghost went through the wall. I went to my bedroom but the ghost went through my bedroom door. Then I woke up (to find) it was all a dream.*

TROUBLESHOOTING

The above weaknesses are common in younger students' writing and many will learn how to construct more satisfactory texts as they gain more experience through reading and writing. There are many older students, however, who still have trouble structuring coherent, well-balanced sentences and who need explicit assistance in such matters as how to:

- compact information into the noun group rather than a string of clauses
- most effectively use simple sentences
- combine clauses in a variety of ways and manage the organisation of longer sentences
- develop compound sentences, complex sentences and compound-complex sentences
- use quoting and reporting sentences
- use commas, semi-colons, colons, parentheses, dashes, inverted commas, and other punctuation to add clarity to more complex sentences.

Explain how authors experiment with the structures of sentences and clauses to create particular effects [Year 9]

Certain texts, such as procedures, need to be very straightforward and easy to read. These texts tend to use simple sentences, consisting of a single clause (ie one message per sentence). Other texts need to use quite lengthy, complex sentences in order to develop a particular line of reasoning or to create connections between ideas in terms of such aspects as time, reason, purpose or manner. With reference to meaning, then, we are interested in such matters as the nature of the relationship between the ideas, the complexity of these relationships, and the clarity with which they are expressed.

Looking at form: Combining items

With regard to form, we are interested in the various ways in which relationships within sentences can be structured. We can combine language items in various ways, from the level of the word, group and phrase through to the clause.

Words and phrases

Words, groups and phrases can be combined using 'joining words' – or conjunctions.

NOUNS AND NOUN GROUPS

cats	and	dogs
big ones	and	little ones
tea	or	coffee

VERBS AND VERB GROUPS

tried	but	failed
huffed	and	puffed
stand up	or	sit down

ADJECTIVES AND ADJECTIVE GROUPS

hot	and	sweaty
tired	but	happy
very sad	although	inevitable

ADVERBS AND ADVERB GROUPS

upstairs	and	downstairs
so calmly	yet	so bravely
sooner	or	later

PREPOSITIONAL PHRASES

up hill	and	down dale
at dawn	and	at dusk
in my mind	and	in my heart

Sometimes we combine two noun groups simply by using one to expand on another:

my neighbour	Mrs Brown ...
Henry VIII,	King of England and Supreme Head of the Church of England ...
Mr. Knightley,	a sensible man about seven or eight-and-thirty ...
noun group	**noun group**

Traditionally, this is referred to as 'nouns in apposition' and is characteristic of more mature writing.

> Understand how higher order concepts are developed in complex texts through language features including nominalisation, apposition and embedding of clauses [Year 10]

Sentences

> ■ identifying and experimenting with a range of clause types and discussing the effect of these in the expression and development of ideas [Year 7]

So far we have been working at the level of the clause and below the clause (groups and words). Here we will look at how clauses are combined in various ways to produce different types of sentences: simple; compound; complex and compound–complex.

Simple sentences

A simple sentence is one that contains a single independent clause – a clause that can stand on its own eg:

> **Place** the seeds in the dirt.
> He **muttered** his apologies.

Notice that in the simple sentences above there is only one verb.

> ■ understanding that a simple sentence expresses a single idea, represented grammatically by a single independent clause (for example 'A kangaroo is a mammal. A mammal suckles its young') [Year 1]

Simple sentences are not necessarily short ones:

> The Dursleys **bought** Dudley and Piers large chocolate ice creams at the entrance.
>
> Pooh always **liked** a little something at eleven o'clock in the morning.

Simple sentences are simple in terms of their structure (ie a single clause), not necessarily in terms of their content:

> A striking quality of this passage, and indeed of this whole volume, **is** its beautifully compressed, poetic language.

The sentence above is a simple sentence consisting of a single clause, but its meaning is not 'simple'.

TROUBLESHOOTING

When considering how many clauses there are in a sentence, it needs to be remembered that embedded clauses don't count as separate clauses. Most embedded clauses are part of the noun group, telling more about the head noun, though they can also modify an adverb (in an adverb group) or an adjective (in an adjective group). (See Chapter 2 p.64)

		NOUN GROUP	
		embedded clause	
Chuang Tzu was	a Chinese philosopher	[[who lived during the 4th century B.C.]]	
There are	so many things	[[to do]].	
Harry tried to remember	the dream	[[he had been having]].	
		ADVERB GROUP	
She ran	so quickly	[[that she was puffed]].	
		ADJECTIVE GROUP	
The shelf was	too high	[[to reach]].	

SIMPLE SENTENCE (SINGLE INDEPENDENT CLAUSE)

Sometimes an embedded clause can function as a Participant. In this case it is still not seen as a clause in its own right but simply part of the larger clause:

embedded clause as Participant	
[[That we are in the midst of crisis]]	is now well understood.
[[To win a championship]]	is my greatest ambition.
[[Eating the oysters]]	was a big mistake.

SIMPLE SENTENCE (SINGLE INDEPENDENT CLAUSE)

Analyse and examine how effective authors control and use a variety of clause structures, including embedded clauses [Year 8]

Combined clauses

Many sentences, however, contain more than one clause – sometimes as many as four or five (and more!), eg:

> Possum **found** a safe tree
> and **climbed** to the farthest branches
> where he **snuggled** into a ball,
> **closed** his weary eyes
> and **fell** asleep.

We can combine clauses in different ways to make different types of sentences:

- compound sentences
- complex sentences, and
- compound–complex sentences

Investigate how clauses can be combined in a variety of ways to elaborate, extend or explain ideas [Year 6]

Compound sentences

Compound sentences consist of two or more independent clauses. Each of these clauses is capable of standing on its own and conveying a message. Each has equal status and provides equally important information. These clauses may be linked together in a sentence using such words as 'and', 'or', 'but', eg:

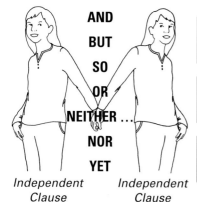

AND
BUT
SO
OR
NEITHER ...
NOR
YET

Independent Clause   Independent Clause

He climbed into bed	**independent clause**
and he fell fast asleep.	**independent clause**

Susan walked home	**independent clause**
but the others caught the bus.	**independent clause**

You could ring him at work	**independent clause**
or you could try him at home.	**independent clause**

Understand that simple connections can be made between ideas by using a compound sentence with two or more clauses and coordinating conjunctions [Year 2]

Words used to combine independent clauses include:

and; so; but; or; yet; and so; not only ... but also; neither ... nor; either ... or

These are called 'coordinators' or 'coordinating conjunctions'.[1]

■ learning how to join simple sentences with conjunctions, for example 'and', 'but' or 'so', to construct compound sentences [Year 2]

Note that, when the Subject of the verb is the same in both clauses, it can be omitted from the second clause:

The ship stopped and [the ship] rolled over on its side.

They all stopped talking and [they] listened.

TROUBLESHOOTING

Students often have trouble knowing how to punctuate compound sentences. A common error is to join them with a comma instead of a conjunction. This is sometimes called a 'comma splice':

✗ *I was late, I caught a taxi.*

✔ *I was late so I caught a taxi.*

---

[1] These are sometimes called 'linkers'.

✔	The Doctor was a very kind man	**but** he hadn't any money.
✔	The King began to tremble	and was very much afraid.
	Independent clause	**Independent clause**

✘	But he hadn't any money	the Doctor was a very kind man.
✘	And was very much afraid	the King began to tremble.
	Independent clause	**Independent clause**

Compound-complex sentences

Some sentences contain a combination of relationships between clauses. These can be referred to as compound-complex sentences.

Two kookaburras flew into the tree	independent clause
and cackled loudly	independent clause
as they scanned the nearby bush for food.	dependent clause

They talked over the new plan	independent clause
while old Hannah cleared the table,	dependent clause
then out came the four little work baskets,	independent clause
and the needles flew	independent clause
as the girls made sheets for Aunt March.	dependent clause

Mrs. Pendyce fixed her eyes upon him,	independent clause
for this was her habit,	independent clause
and she thought	independent clause
how she would run up to town alone	dependent clause
when the spring came again,	dependent clause
and stay at Green's Hotel,	independent clause
where she had always stayed with her father	dependent clause
when she was a girl.	dependent clause

TROUBLESHOOTING

Sometimes the conjunction is omitted and the relationship between clauses remains implicit, eg:

> Sally was fuming. She had been omitted from the team. All she could think of was revenge.

In this case, students have to be able to infer the relationship, eg:

*Sally was fuming **because** [reason] she had been omitted from the team
so [result] all she could think of was revenge.*

These hidden relationships are not always easy for some students to retrieve.

Quoting and reporting

There is another way in which we can combine messages. When we use saying
verbs and sensing verbs, we often include a clause (or clauses) indicating what was
said or sensed.

Investigate how quoted (direct) and reported (indirect) speech work in different types of text
[Year 4]

Quoting

In some cases, we quote the actual words said or thought.

"What's the matter?"	**quoted clause (actual words)**
asked Andrew.	**quoting clause**

The girl cried:	**quoting clause**
"Apple tree, please hide us!"	**quoted clause (actual words)**

"Eat one of my crab-apples,"	**quoted clause (actual words)**
the tree answered,	**quoting clause**
"and I will tell you."	**quoted clause (actual words)**

"There is nothing to worry about,"	**quoted clause (actual words)**
Maria thought to herself.	**quoting clause**

This is often referred to as 'direct speech'.

Reporting

Rather than quoting the exact words, we sometimes report what was said or thought.

I told him	**reporting clause**
that I was sorry.	**reported clause**

She said	**reporting clause**
she never wanted to see him again.	**reported clause**

They thought	**reporting clause**
it was rather odd.	**reported clause**

This is called 'indirect speech'.

Both quoting and reporting are found in text types such as newspaper articles, stories, advertisements, biographies and recounts.

- investigating examples of quoted (direct) speech ('He said, "I'll go to the park today".') and reported (indirect) speech ('He told me he was going to the park today.') and comparing similarities and differences [Year 4]

In terms of meaning, students might be encouraged to think about why a writer would choose either to use a direct quote or to report indirectly what has been said (See also Chapter 4 p.114). They might also reflect on how quoting and reporting on what characters say, think and feel in a narrative can help build up the character and give insights into their motivations, reflections, intentions or desires. When reading and writing expository texts, students might discuss such issues as when it is appropriate to quote someone, why you would select a particular authority to quote, how quoting can add weight to an argument, and the difference between citing, paraphrasing, and plagiarising.

TROUBLESHOOTING

In terms of accuracy, students need to know how to punctuate quoted speech and reported speech. Quoted speech in particular can cause difficulty for some students. In stories, for example, they need to know about using a comma (or question mark or exclamation mark) before the speech mark, about where to place the quoting clause, about when to use single speech marks and double speech marks. In expository writing, students need to know how to quote authorities they are referring to (eg within the body of the text for a short quote; as a separate indented paragraph for a longer quote) and how to reference these quotes.

Other types of clauses

Non-finite clauses

In creating complex sentences, we can also use a non-finite dependent clause.

You can get immediate help	independent clause
by dialling the emergency number.	dependent clause

To make vegetable soup,	dependent clause
you will need a clear broth.	independent clause

A non-finite clause is a 'stripped back' clause, usually without an explicit Subject (eg *you*), modality or tense (eg as carried in an auxiliary such as *could* or *was*) or subordinating conjunction (eg *as*). Generally, you can 'translate' a non-finite clause into its finite form by re-inserting such features, eg:

NON-FINITE

They crawled to the top of the hill **to see** *the surrounding landscape.*

FINITE

They crawled to the top of the hill **so that** *[+ conjunction]* **they** *[+ Subject]* **could** *[+ modality]* **see** *the surrounding landscape.*

NON-FINITE

Sitting *alone in her bedroom, she began to think of what had happened.*

FINITE

As *[+ conjunction]* **she** *[+ Subject]* **sat** *[+ tense] alone in her bedroom, she began to think of what had happened.*

NON-FINITE

Shocked *by the news, they hurried to the hospital.*

FINITE

Because *[+ conjunction]* **they** *[+ Subject]* **were** *[+ tense]* **shocked** *by the news, they hurried to the hospital.*

Note the different forms of non-finite clauses in the sentences above:

'to –' clauses

'– ing' clauses

'– ed' clauses

As we have seen earlier, non-finite clauses can also be embedded in the noun group[5] as a Qualifier to provide more information about the thing in question:

At the end of the street is <u>*a hotel [[perched on the cliff]]*</u>*.*

Opposite the hotel is <u>*a scenic path [[overlooking the gateway to the Sydney Harbour]]*</u>*.*

This is <u>*the perfect spot [[to watch the colourful array of yachts in full sail]]*</u>*.*

Non-finite clauses are more economical, characteristic of the 'compacted' nature of written language. The use of non-finite clauses is typically a sign of greater maturity and students should be encouraged to observe and employ them where appropriate.

The following excerpts from a chapter of *Alice in Wonderland* contains several examples of non-finite clauses:

> The Hatter was the first **[[to break the silence]]**. 'What day of the month is it?' he said, **turning to Alice**: he had taken his watch out of his pocket, and was looking at it uneasily, **shaking it every now and then, and holding it to his ear**.
>
> The Dormouse shook its head impatiently, and said, **without opening its eyes**, 'Of course, of course; just what I was going to remark myself.'
>
> 'Have you guessed the riddle yet?' the Hatter said, **turning to Alice again**.
>
> The Dormouse again took a minute or two **[[to think about it]]**.

---

[5]   They can also be embedded in an adjective group (*We were happy [[to wander]] all day.*).

'What did they draw?' said Alice, **quite forgetting her promise**.

'Treacle,' said the Dormouse, **without considering at all this time**.

This answer so confused poor Alice, that she let the Dormouse go on for some time **without interrupting it**.

'They were learning **to draw**,' the Dormouse went on, **yawning and rubbing its eyes**, for it was getting very sleepy.

She began **by taking the little golden key**, and **unlocking the door that led into the garden**. Then she went to work **nibbling at the mushroom**.

Interrupting clauses

Sometimes, one clause interrupts another.[6] Instead of saying, for example: *And then she slipped away* **without saying a word**, the writer might insert '*without saying a word*' inside the previous clause: *And then,* **without saying a word***, she slipped away.*

Note how interrupting clauses are usually divided off by commas.

Here are a few more examples, taken from *Love Among the Chickens* by P.G. Wodehouse:

Mr. Beale, **having carefully deposited the gun against the wall and dropped a pair of very limp rabbits on the floor**, proceeded to climb in through the window.

It had always been my experience that, **when Ukridge was around**, things began to happen swiftly and violently.

"This," **said Ukridge, leaning against the door and endeavouring to button his collar at the back**, "reminds me of an afternoon in the Argentine."

Aunty, **still clutching a much-bitten section of a beef sandwich**, was breathing heavily.

Sometimes it is prepositional phrases, rather than clauses, that interrupt:

We, **in the meantime**, were chasing the rest of the birds all over the garden.

On my return, I found Ukridge, **in his shirt sleeves and minus a collar**, assailing a large ham.

---

6   These are also called 'enclosed clauses'.

Interrupting clauses and phrases are often used in order to change the emphasis or for stylistic reasons. They do, however, break the flow of the text and require concentration on the reader's part. Consider, for example, what challenges the following sentences containing multiple interruptions might pose for the casual or inexperienced reader as the following excerpts from *Love Among the Chickens* by P.G. Wodehouse:

> What I wanted, **to enable me to give the public of my best (as the reviewer of a weekly paper, dealing with my last work, had expressed a polite hope that I would continue to do)** was a little haven in the country somewhere.
>
> …
>
> The bustle of the platform had increased momentarily, until now, **when, from the snorting of the engine, it seemed likely that the train might start at any minute**, the crowd's excitement was extreme.
>
> …
>
> The red-headed Beale, **discovered leaning in an attitude of thought on the yard gate and observing the feathered mob below with much interest**, was roused from his reflections and despatched to the town for the wire and sugar boxes.

This last example of interrupting clauses is from *The Avalanche* by G.F.H. Atherton:

> The vast ruin, **with its tottering arches and broken columns, its lonely walls looking as if bitten by prehistoric monsters that must haunt this ancient coast, the soft pastel colours the great fire had given as sole compensation for all it had taken, the grotesque twisted masses of steel and the aged grey hills that had looked down on so many fires**, had appealed powerfully to his imagination.

Relative clauses

We have already met relative clauses when we were looking at the noun group (eg **The woman *that I met at the party*** *is Sarah's grandmother*). Such clauses are embedded in the noun group, functioning as Qualifiers that provide further information about the thing in question and usually specifying 'which one'. For this reason, they are sometimes called 'defining relative clauses'.

There is, however, another kind of relative clause. These simply add a bit of extra information – they don't specify which thing is being spoken about and are not part of the noun group. These are called 'non-defining relative clauses'. They are generally separated off by commas.

> Her mouth was large and so were her eyes, **which looked green in some lights and moods and grey in others.**
>
> Marilla lighted a candle and told Anne to follow her, **which Anne spiritlessly did.**
>
> And she is good and smart, **which is better than being pretty.**
>
> *Anne of Green Gables*, L.M. Montgomery

Look at the difference, for example, between these two sentences.

> *My sister* **who lives in Parramatta** *is coming to visit next week.* (Answers 'Which one?')

> *My sister,* **who lives in Parramatta,** *is coming to visit next week.* (Provides some additional information.)

Both of these are relative clauses, but their meaning is quite different. In the first example, the relative clause is defining which sister we are referring to (ie 'the sister who lives in Parramatta') – a 'defining relative clause'. In the second example, the commas indicate that the relative clause is simply adding some non-essential information – a 'non-defining relative clause'.

TROUBLESHOOTING

In their reading, many learners experience difficulties in comprehending these less 'standard' types of clauses. It is worth spending time reading aloud passages containing such clauses, using intonation to indicate boundaries and chunks. Students also need demonstrations of how to read sentences carefully in order to identify relationships between ideas, rather than skimming quickly through a text. In their writing, they might need support in constructing sentences that create increasingly complex meanings and yet retain their clarity.

Combining clauses: Monitoring student learning

Young learners

- When listening and reading, can students comprehend a relatively wide range of clause combinations?

- When reading to students, would it be useful for the teacher to model the 'meaning units' (clauses) within sentences through intonation and pausing?

- Can they identify short and long sentences, the number of 'ideas' contained within a sentence, and any words that join the ideas?

- Can they point out the punctuation signalling the beginning and end of a sentence?

- Are they using compound sentences in their writing?

- Are they starting to use some complex sentences in written texts, for example recounts containing 'time clauses' (*'When we got home, I fell asleep.'*)?

Later primary

- Are students comprehending and employing a wide variety of sentence types (compound, complex, compound–complex, as well as quoting and reporting sentences) in both their spoken and written language?

- Do they need help with sentences in their written texts that are overly long and rambling, overly short and stilted, awkwardly structured, or poorly punctuated?

- Are they learning how to use quoting and reporting (direct and indirect speech) and how to punctuate quoted speech and thoughts?

- Can they discuss when and why to use quoting and reporting sentences?

- In their reading, are students being exposed to texts that provide models of richly patterned sentences?

- If a class text proves to be challenging, are students introduced to strategies for 'unpacking' the text (eg seeing it in terms of 'meaning units'; identifying the relationship between units/clauses; unravelling lengthy noun groups).

- Can they identify basic examples of simple, compound and complex sentences?

- Can they talk about how different types of common conjunctions join ideas in various ways (eg time, cause, adding information)?

Older learners

- Are students' written texts (and prepared oral presentations) differentiated from their more spontaneous spoken language, demonstrating a more crafted quality?

- Are they using structures such as embedded clauses and nouns in apposition to make their writing more compact?

- Is careful and informed reworking of sentences a regular feature of their writing practices (including relevant aspects of punctuation: commas; semicolons; colons; dashes; parentheses)?

- Is there evidence of students using a wide range of dependent clauses (eg time, manner, cause, condition, concession) appropriately, extending their ability to make increasingly complex connections between ideas?

- Are they able to identify, in broad terms, different types of sentences (simple, compound, complex and compound–complex) and to recognise different types of relationships between clauses as signalled by conjunctions?

- Do their texts include a variety of well-selected simple, compound, complex and compound–complex sentences, depending on the text type?

- Do their sentences display a range of clause types (dependent/ independent; finite/non-finite; defining relative clauses/non-defining relative clauses; interrupting clauses) – as appropriate?

- Are they able to reflect on and discuss the selection of different sentence types in terms of how they contribute to the meaning, impact and flow of the text?

- Are quoting and reporting sentences used effectively, with accurate punctuation, in texts such as stories, biographies, historical recounts, and exposition?

- Are they aware of the difference between quoting, reporting, paraphrasing and plagiarism?

- Are they learning how to cite an author in an expository text and provide an adequate reference?

- In their reading, are they able to comprehend sentences containing more challenging relationships signalled by such subordinating conjunctions as: *although*; *in spite of*; *even if*; *while, unless*?

- Are they able to interpret the meaning of sentences that contain interrupting clauses and phrases?

- Can they understand the difference in meaning between defining and non-defining relative clauses?

Connecting ideas: analysed texts

The following texts have been analysed to provide examples of different kinds of clauses and how they can be combined. This is not to suggest that students should be asked to analyse a text in this way.

- Embedded clauses are indicated by double square brackets [[...]].

- Division between clauses is indicated by double slashes // where appropriate.

- Interrupting clauses are indicated by double angle brackets « ... ».

- Groups that include embeddings are underlined.

Two texts have been analysed – a simple historical recount by a 7-year-old student and an historical exposition by a 15-year-old student. Apart from providing examples of analysed sentences, the texts demonstrate the increasing complexity over the years of schooling, from the relatively basic sentences of early primary school through to the advanced relationships between clauses expected of students in secondary school.

TEXT A: SENTENCE TYPES IN AN HISTORICAL RECOUNT WRITTEN BY A 7-YEAR-OLD

SIMPLE SENTENCE	
One day in 1888 a ship **crashed** onto the reef near Queensland.	**single independent clause**

SIMPLE SENTENCE	
It **was carried** onto the reef by a swift current.	**single independent clause**

COMPOUND SENTENCE	
A baby **was born** the same day	independent clause
and its crying **reached** the ears of the fearful sailors.	independent clause
SIMPLE SENTENCE	
It **was floating** on a large board in the ocean.	single independent clause
COMPLEX SENTENCE	
The sailors **knew**	independent clause (reporting)
they **could not reach** the baby.	dependent clause ('what was reported')

TEXT B: SENTENCE TYPES IN AN HISTORICAL EXPOSITION WRITTEN BY A 15-YEAR-OLD

Assess the impact of World War II on women's lives and roles.

SIMPLE SENTENCE	
Women's lives and roles in Australian society **were changed** irreversibly by WWII.	single independent clause
COMPLEX SENTENCE	
As Darlington **points out**,	dependent clause (reporting)
many women **demanded**	independent clause (reporting)
to be involved in the War effort more directly [[than they had been allowed in previous Wars]].	dependent clause ('what was reported') – using a non-finite clause) – includes an adverb group with an embedded clause
SIMPLE SENTENCE	
Women **joined** voluntary organisations [[where they learned new skills [[that would be valuable // if the War reached Australia]]]].	independent clause – includes a noun group with embedded clauses
COMPLEX SENTENCE	
Although they **were paid** little more than half the wages [[paid to men // for doing the same job]],	dependent clause (concessive) – includes a noun group with two embedded clauses
women in cities **worked** in factories and steel mills,	independent clause
while their rural counterparts **took on** shearing, dairying, crop planting and harvesting.	dependent clause (contrastive)

SIMPLE SENTENCE	
*Interestingly, Darlington **mentions** an issue regarding <u>the opposition [[women encountered in their fight for equality]]</u>.*	independent clause – includes a noun group with an embedded clause
COMPLEX SENTENCE	
*He **says***	independent clause (reporting)
*that « although the Government **used** extensive propaganda recruitment campaigns to **encourage** women **to join** the workforce and service »,* *this great change in traditional gender roles **encountered** hostility from sections of society at the time.*	dependent clause ('what is reported') – interrupted by other dependent clauses
SIMPLE SENTENCE	
*These **include** the media, the Catholic Church, and <u>some men [[who feared a reduction in their wages]]</u>.*	single clause – includes a noun group with an embedded clause
COMPOUND SENTENCE	
*The service experience **had** a profoundly liberating effect on many women,*	independent clause
*and after the War some **sought** <u>jobs [[that would continue their independence and liberation]]</u>.*	independent clause – includes a noun group with an embedded clause
SIMPLE SENTENCE	
*Many **had** <u>problems [[giving up the responsibility [[the War had given them]]]]</u>.*	single clause – includes embeddings
COMPLEX SENTENCE	
*Others, however, **were** <u>happy [[to return to the 'normality' of domestic life]]</u>*	independent clause – includes an adjective group with an embedded clause
*when the War **ended**.*	dependent clause (time)
COMPLEX SENTENCE	
*Finally, Darlington **explains***	independent clause (reporting)
*how women's independence **was taken away** from them by the Government, Catholic Church and media*	dependent clause ('what was reported')
*as the War **drew** to a close.*	dependent clause (time)

COMPLEX SENTENCE	
He says	**independent clause** (reporting)
*that it is clear [[that women **were expected** // **to return** to their traditional gender and family roles, //whether they **wished** to or not]].*	**dependent clause** ('what was reported')

COMPLEX SENTENCE	
It seems	**independent clause**
*that « even though women **had made** a huge contribution to the war effort », there **would be** no change in social attitudes.*	**dependent clause** – interrupted by another dependent clause (concession)

4 Language for interacting with others

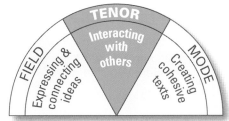

We have been looking at how we use language to express and connect ideas in representing our experience of the world. Another major function of language is to enable us to interact in the world. This is referred to as the 'interpersonal' function of language – how language is used to foster social interaction, to create and maintain relationships, to develop and project a personal identity, to express opinions and engage with the views of others.

In any context we take up different roles and build different kinds of relationships. This results in a certain tenor. The tenor will influence the kinds of interpersonal language choices made in any particular situation.

> ■ learning that language varies according to the relationships between people, for example between parent and child, teacher and student, siblings, friends, shopkeepers and customers [Foundation]

> Understand that patterns of language interaction vary across social contexts and types of texts and that they help to signal social roles and relationships [Year 5]

> Understand that strategies for interaction become more complex and demanding as levels of formality and social distance increase [Year 6]

There is great subtlety in the way in which humans interact and the language system has evolved to cope with these complex ways of relating to each other, including the use of facial expression, body language and intonation.

> Understand that language is used in combination with other means of communication, for example facial expressions and gestures to interact with others [Year 1]

The interpersonal dimension is being increasingly recognised as important in creating the conditions for learning and for critical awareness. While teachers are often hesitant to intervene in students' interpersonal language development, it is possible to extend their repertoire by deliberately modelling effective language use, drawing their attention to relevant features and explicitly teaching a range of interpersonal strategies.

In this chapter, we will first look at how we use statements, questions, commands and offers in our interactions with others. The following sections[1] deal with how

---

[1] These sections draw on Appraisal Theory, developed primarily by James Martin and Peter White within the context of Halliday's functional theory of language.

by the base form of the verb). It is now possible to reverse the Subject and the 'invented' auxiliary.

She **likes** *pasta.* → *She* **does** *like pasta.* → **Does she** *like pasta?*

They **went** *to Wagga.* → *They* **did go** *to Wagga.* → **Did they** *go to Wagga?*

Sometimes we simply use a rising intonation to indicate a question.

She likes pasta?

When we want confirmation, we can use a 'tag question'.

She likes pasta, doesn't she?

TROUBLESHOOTING

It is not important to teach the structure of questions, as most native speakers of English will be using them quite comfortably without explicit instruction. ESL learners, however, often have problems with the structure of questions, and you might need to be able to demonstrate how to construct them in English.

The type of question above is generally called a 'yes/no' or closed question. These are the most limiting type of question, requiring a simple 'yes' or 'no' answer. We can also ask 'wh-' questions such as *'Who?'*, *'When?'*, *'Where?'*. These have a somewhat different structure and function. They still ask for information, but require an answer that goes beyond a simple yes or no. Wh- questions are referred to as open questions and encourage a wider range of responses. Some types of 'wh-' questions result in a relatively constrained answer, usually supplying a specific piece of information (for example, *'When did you arrive?'*; *'Where did you go?'*). Others (eg 'Why?' and 'How?') often provoke a lengthier, more complex response, allowing for a much greater exploration of ideas (for example, *'Why do you think he did that?'*; *'How did you work that out?'*).

Question Type	Question	Possible Response
'yes/no' 'wh-'	*Did they go to Wagga?* *When did they leave?* *Why did they go?*	Yes. *At 8 o'clock.* *Because John's father was sick and they wanted to see how he was doing.*

- learning about different types of questions including closed and open questions and 'where', 'what', 'who' and 'why' questions [Year 1]

Interrogative words such as *who, whom, whose, what* and *which* are used when we want to ask a wh- question.

Who knows the answer?

To *whom* did you send it?

Whose umbrella is this?

What can you see?

Which do you prefer?

When did she leave?

Where did she go?

Why did she leave?

How do you know?

The structure of commands

The typical structure of a command is quite simple – we just use the base form of the verb, generally omitting the Subject.[6]

Answer the phone.

Leave me alone.

Be quiet!

You *go* first.

There is also a special case where the construction **Let's** is used to suggest a course of action:

Let's pretend to be rabbits.

Negative statements, questions and commands

It's relatively easy to make statements and questions negative, simply by adding 'not' after the auxiliary.

Positive	Negative
He has left.	*He has not left.*
Has he left?	*Hasn't he left?*

However, there is a problem if no auxiliary exists to which to attach the 'not'. So, again, it will be necessary to 'invent' a dummy auxiliary: *do/does* or *did*, used with the base form of the verb.

	Positive	Negative
Simple present tense	*It stings.*	*It **does** **not** sting.*
Simple past tense	*It stung.*	*It **didn't** sting.*

Similarly, when making commands negative, it will be necessary to insert an auxiliary:

Positive command	Negative command
Hurry!	***Don't** hurry!*

---

[6] This is called the Imperative Mood.

Exclamations

We use exclamations to express surprise or make an emphatic statement. In structuring exclamations in the written mode, we can just use a statement followed by an exclamation mark.

> *He's so generous!*

> *We had a great time!*

Sometimes we use an expression such as How + adjective! or What + noun group!.

> *How strange!*

> *What idiots!*

Students can explore different ways of using emphasis in their oral and written language – particularly in dramatic presentations, stories and poems, including how it can be used for sarcasm and irony.

Involvement

When we interact with others, we generally seek to establish a sense of solidarity. In doing so, we use resources such as speech role pronouns, terms of address and language that can either include or exclude others.

Speech role pronouns

One of the most obvious resources used in interaction are the speech role pronouns (that is, first and second person pronouns – *I, me, my, we, us, our* and *you, your*). While this hardly seems worth mentioning, it can in fact be significant.

> ■ identifying the use of first person (I, we) and second person pronouns (you) to distance or involve the audience, for example in a speech made to a local cultural community [Year 10]

We could ask how the pronouns are being used to develop relationships – between the speaker and listener, between the reader and writer, or between different participants in the text. Is the reader addressed as 'you'? Why/why not? Does the writer identify herself or himself as 'I'? What is the effect of this? Is 'we' used to include the audience? We can play around with these resources to create a feeling of solidarity (for example, the poem/song by Woodley & Newton, 'I am, you are, we are Australians'). Such strategies are often used in advertising to encourage a sense of connection and compliance in the buyer or client. We also find them used in children's books. In this extract, for example, we can see how the writer is trying to engage the reader by using personal pronouns:

> Of all the beautiful insects **we** see from time to time in gardens, in parks, or during **our** rambles in the countryside, none would appear to have the same attraction for **us** as do the butterflies and moths. Because these insects are so highly favoured, **I** am giving them first place and dealing with them at length, but before **we** go on to the more practical side of the work **I** will discuss briefly the subject of English and scientific names and life-history, as this will enable **you** to have a better understanding of what is to follow ... Let **me** tell **you** at once that **you** have absolutely no need whatever to be alarmed by scientific names. In fact **I** advise **you** to make use of them on all occasions, as by doing so they will soon be second nature to **you**.
>
> C.V.A. Adams

TROUBLESHOOTING

ESL learners often come from language backgrounds with quite different systems of speech role pronouns. There might be different ways of referring to someone depending on their status, (for example, tu and Lei in Italian) or number (eg Du (singular 'you') and Sie (plural 'you') in German). In Indonesian, there are different ways of referring to 'we' – kami and kita – depending on whether you are including the person spoken to or not.

Terms of address

Terms of address[7] are an important resource in establishing and maintaining relationships in terms of power, status, familiarity, and feelings. They indicate our relationship to the person or help to position them in a particular role. These are generally noun groups such as titles, nicknames, terms of endearment, or proper names (eg *'Hello* **Mrs McNaught***'; 'Come here,* **Tommy***'; 'Yes sir'; 'G'day* **Jacko***'; 'Okay darling'; 'Certainly* **Your Worship***'*). We often take such matters for granted, but we are regularly placed in situations where we have to make decisions about how to refer to people. Do we use their title (Mr Brown)? At what point can you use their given name (Garry)? Could you use a nickname (Gazza)? In which contexts can you use it? Do you call your in-laws 'Mum' and 'Dad'? What intimate or 'pet' names might you use with your spouse and children (Honey dumpling)?

- exploring how terms of address are used to signal different kinds of relationships [Year 2]

Look at how carefully Kipling uses terms of address to define roles and relationships in the *Just So Stories*: the independent Cat addresses the human as 'O my Enemy and Wife of my Enemy' while the more submissive Bat calls her 'O my Hostess and wife of my Host' and the tamed horse now refers to her as 'O my Mistress and Wife of my Master'. Kipling himself directly engages with his child-reader by using the term of endearment 'Best Beloved'.

Students might consider how 'what you call someone' helps to establish a particular type of relationship – from the name you call your pet (Lucky) right through to

---

[7] These are sometimes called 'vocatives'.

the most powerful titles (Your Honour, Your Majesty). They might also think about negative name-calling such as 'pimple face', 'dog', 'slut', 'drama queen' and 'bitch'. Terms of address can function to create in-group solidarity (eg nicknames) or exclusion (eg derogatory names).

'In group' and 'out group'

Understand how language use can have inclusive and exclusive social effects, and can empower or disempower people [Year 10]

■ reflecting on experiences of when language includes, distances or marginalises others [Year 10]

Members of a discourse community often use varieties of language that can have the effect of being 'inclusive' or 'exclusive'. Such language can include the use of technical terminology, slang, swearing, and so on. By using the language of the 'group', we can build up solidarity and group cohesion. At the same time, we can exclude others from participation in the group.

■ recognising the importance of using inclusive language [Year 4]

Typical examples of 'in-group' language include the jargon associated with rapping, with fashion, with geeks and nerds, and with the various football codes. Similarly, the ability to understand the technicality of the various disciplines will create insiders and outsiders.

■ identifying the various communities to which students belong and how language reinforces membership of these communities (the intimate language of family members, the jargon of teenage groups, the technicality of some online communities, the language specific to recreational groups, the interaction patterns of the classroom, the commonalities in migrant and cultural groups) [Year 9]

Humour is often used to engage with others and reinforce group boundaries – who understands the joke and who doesn't? Word play, irony, sarcasm, jokes and humorous insults feature, for example, in the friendship talk of preadolescent girls where they are seeking to build alliances.

Expressing attitudes

One way to stimulate interaction is to talk about our feelings and opinions. Such attitudinal language generally invites a response from the listener or reader.

■ comparing texts that use evaluative language in different ways – print advertisements, editorials, talkback radio and poetry – and identifying wordings that appraise things indirectly, through evocative language, similes and metaphors that direct the views of the readers in particular ways [Year 9]

The expression of human feelings, emotions, opinions and judgements is very rich and complex and involves delicate language choices. We need to consider how these choices are going to be influenced by the particular context. In the context of gossiping, for example, we might expect lots of 'attitudinal language' – often negative – appraising someone's looks or behaviour. In the context of an academic essay, the choices will be concerned with more subtle critique of ideas and research.

■ exploring examples of language which demonstrate a range of feelings and positions, and building a vocabulary to express judgments about characters or events, acknowledging that language and judgments might differ depending on the cultural context [Year 3]

We also need to look at how the attitudinal language builds up through the text. Is the tone set at the beginning of the text (spoken or written)? Does it change over the course of the text? How does the tone influence the way in which subsequent utterances are interpreted?

Students need to be able to identify when a text is attempting to persuade them to a particular point of view or position them in a particular way. This often happens through the language choices made by the speaker or writer (eg obsession, mongrel, eyesore, monstrosity, cult). Persuasive language might be more obvious in text types that seek to influence (eg exposition, advertisements, editorials, stories) but can also occur less obviously in more 'objective' text types.

Understand differences between the language of opinion and the language of factual reporting or recording [Year 4]

In expressing attitudes about things and behaviour, we are constructing ourselves and others in a particular way. It is through such language that we represent ourselves as being intelligent, cool, discerning, concerned, honest, humble, and so on. On a broader level, such values construct our relationships with family and friends. And ultimately, the sum total of such attitudes and behaviours construct social, cultural and ideological values.

■ understanding that our use of language helps to create different identities, for example teenage groups and sportspeople have adopted particular words or ways of speaking [Year 8]

Understand that roles and relationships are developed and challenged through language interpersonal skills [Year 9]

Here we will look at three main kinds of attitudinal language:

1 Describing emotions and how people feel ('affect'):[8]
  *The children are **very upset**.*

2 Evaluating the worth and quality of things and processes ('appreciation'):
  *What a **lovely** film!*

3 Making judgements about people's behaviour ('judgement'):
  *She such **a fibber**!*

---

[8] Here 'affect' is used as a noun, with the stress on the first syllable: affect.

■ building a knowledge base about words of evaluation, including words to express emotional responses to texts, judgment of characters and their actions, and appreciation of the aesthetic qualities of text [Year 7]

Words that express attitudes can be 'positive' (eg *good*) or 'negative' (eg *bad*).

	POSITIVE	NEGATIVE
expressing emotions ('affect')	happy happiness happily	sad sadness sadly
appreciating things ('appreciation')	beautiful beauty	ugly ugliness
judging behaviour ('judgement')	clever cleverness cleverly	stupid stupidity stupidly

Expressing feelings

When we interact with others, we often talk about how we feel. When we express emotions the listener or reader might agree or disagree, might question or argue, might be empathetic or scornful.

Investigate how vocabulary choices, including evaluative language can express shades of meaning, feeling and opinion [Year 6]

We can talk about different kinds of emotions, for example:

1 *'matters of the heart' – happiness/unhappiness (eg sadness, love, anger, excitement)*
She was **ecstatic**.
They **laughed** a lot.

2 *'pursuit of goals' – satisfaction/ dissatisfaction (eg curiosity, respect, displeasure, satisfaction)*
I'm **feeling bored**.
They **enjoyed** themselves.

3 *'social wellbeing' – security/ insecurity (eg feeling safe, secure, anxious, fearful, confident)*
I'm **afraid**.
What a **tragedy**!

When emotions are expressed, whether spoken or written, they can be the emotions of the speaker or writer (*I can't stand him!*) or they can be emotions attributed to others (*Kathy was distraught.*).

Understand that language can be used to explore ways of expressing needs, likes and dislikes [Foundation]

When we talk about emotions, we use nouns and adjectives, verbs and adverbs:

	POSITIVE	NEGATIVE
nouns	love	fear
adjectives	happy	miserable
verbs	adore	hate
adverbs	cheerfully	sadly

Feelings can be expressed directly as emotional states (happiness) or implied indirectly through physical actions (cried).

When seeking to express feelings in a more detached ways, nominalisation can be used. Instead of using an adjective, for example, a noun group can be used:

> I felt a bit **sad** → I felt **a twinge of sadness**.
>
> I was **scared** → **Fear** gripped me.

Explore different ways of expressing emotions, including verbal, visual, body language and facial expressions [Year 1]

- extending students' vocabularies for the expression of feelings and emotions [Year 1]

Evaluating the qualities of things

As well as responding emotionally to something, we can express an opinion about the qualities of something (eg artworks, ideas, clothing, bodies, food, utensils), evaluating such aspects as:

1 their **composition** or aesthetic value – are they well structured, symmetrical, of pleasing colour or shape, jarring, incomplete and so on? The value will depend on individual taste, social norms and cultural preferences.

> She looked very **elegant**.
>
> It's a **complex** puzzle.
>
> The plot was **not well developed**.

Identify language that can be used for appreciating texts and the qualities of people and things [Year 2]

2 their **social value** or worth/significance – are they useful, important, irrelevant, cutting-edge and so on? Such values are obviously important in developing ideological positions.

> It's a **significant** breakthrough.
>
> You have a **valid** argument.

3 the **reaction** they provoke – particularly in terms of the impact that something has or a quality that it possesses. Reaction is easily confused with 'affect' (above). But whereas 'affect' is concerned with the expression of subjective emotions, with the emphasis on the person and their feelings, (eg *I am bored*), 'impact' is more concerned with the phenomenon producing the feeling (eg *the film was boring*).

*The exhibition was **fascinating**.*

*It was a **terrifying** movie.*

■ identifying (for example from reviews) the ways in which evaluative language is used to assess the qualities of the various aspects of the work in question [Year 6]

	POSITIVE	NEGATIVE
composition	well-built intricate symmetrical	contradictory broken unbalanced
social value	victory worthy success	inefficient insignificant unfair
reaction	delicious impressive heartwarming	exhausting worry disappointing

Examining the language of appreciation is particularly important in regard to literary texts: How do the authors employ evaluative language in developing, for example, the characters and setting? How do reviewers use the language of appraisal to evaluate literary texts?

Understand how language is used to evaluate texts and how evaluations about a text can be substantiated by reference to the text and other sources [Year 7]

Understand that people's evaluations of texts are influenced by their value systems, the context and the purpose and mode of communication [Year 10]

Judging human behaviour

Our attitudes might include opinions about people's behaviour (what they do, say or believe). We can praise, admire, criticise or condemn their actions.

■ distinguishing how choice of adverbs, nouns and verbs present different evaluations of characters in texts [Year 3]

Sometimes people's behaviour is nominalised (ie turned into an abstract 'thing', eg *rudeness = behaving in a rude way*). In such cases we need to recognise that we are still judging behaviour, not evaluating a thing (as above).

■ exploring in stories, everyday and media texts moral and social dilemmas; such as right and wrong, fairness/unfairness, inclusion and exclusion [Year 2]

We can judge behaviour in terms of:

1 social esteem – involving personal and psychological factors:

■ Is he or she special in some way ('normality')?

He's always been **an eccentric**.

Bizarrely, he rejoiced at the news.

■ Does she or he have a particular ability ('capacity/competence')?

Her **intelligence** is not being questioned.

As a manager, he was grossly **incompetent**.

■ Is he or she reliable ('tenacity/resolve')?

She **worked tirelessly** for charity.

They are just **lazy**.

2 social sanction – involving behaviour with moral, ethical or legal implications:

■ Is he or she honest ('veracity')?

We discussed the matter **openly and frankly**.

Nixon was **devious**.

■ Is he or she ethical ('propriety')?

We see ourselves as **the peacekeepers**.

She's just **a gossip**.

■ reflecting on experiences of when language includes, distances or marginalises others [Year 10]

It is important to note that expressions of attitude can be explicit or implicit. We could say, for example, 'She was very **kind**.' – explicitly referring to a quality (social esteem). Or we could have said 'She made me a cup of tea and listened while I talked.'. Here there is no overt expression of attitude, but we could infer from her behaviour that she acted in a kind way. In order to make such an inference, we would need to understand the context – firstly the cultural context (in which such behaviour could be construed as 'kind') and secondly the textual context, where the preceding text would have oriented us to 'read' the rest of the text in a particular way (ie that she was acting kindly).

Investigate how evaluation can be expressed directly and indirectly using devices, for example allusion, evocative vocabulary and metaphor [Year 9]

Adjusting strength and focus

In the previous section we explored how we use language to construct a rich and varied array of emotions and opinions.

Another interpersonal language resource is to boost or lower the strength of our messages. I could, for example, say:

> *I'm worried.*

I could raise the intensity by adding an 'intensifier':[9]

> *I'm **really** worried.*

Or I could lower the intensity:

> *I'm **a bit** worried.*

> ■ exploring how language is used to express feelings including learning vocabulary to express a gradation of feeling, for example 'happy', 'joyful', 'pleased', 'contented' [Year 2]

In this way, I am grading the strength of the message. We refer to this strategy as Graduation. The Graduation system works closely with Attitude (and with Engagement to a certain extent).

> Examine how evaluative language can be varied to be more or less forceful [Year 3]

There are two main ways in which we use this resource:

- ▪ to increase or decrease the **force** of the message
- ▪ to sharpen or soften the **focus** of the message.

Force

We can increase or decrease the force of a message by using:

- ▪ adverbs
  eg *I'm feeling **slightly** sick.*

- ▪ adjectives,
  eg *You're a **complete** fool.*

- ▪ nouns
  eg *What a **stink**!*

- ▪ verbs
  eg *I **adore** strawberries.*

All of these can be graded along a cline, from least intense to most intense.

Least intense		→		**Most intense**
slightly	*somewhat*	→	*very*	*extremely*
homely	*plain*	→	*good-looking*	*gorgeous*

Notice how we can change the intensity by adding an intensifier:

[9] See also 'intensifiers' in Chapter 2.

She was *a bit* → *rather* → *very* → *extremely* irritated.

Or by changing the force of the vocabulary item itself:

She was *irritated* → *annoyed* → *angered* → *furious*.

Here are some more examples of intensifiers:

terribly	just	really	awfully	somewhat
deeply	dreadfully	half	incredibly	moderately
certainly	so	surely	obviously	plainly
nearly	quite	scarcely	practically	sort of
utterly	wonderfully	truly	reasonably	drastically
partly	perfectly	poorly	slightly	soundly
kind of	more or less	hardly	very	extremely
absolutely	rather	fairly	virtually	entirely
generally	typically	by and large	basically	overall
much	more	less	(the) most	(the) least
better	(the) best	worse	(the) worst	more or less

We can also boost the force of a message by repeating:

eg I'm *very, very* angry.

He *struggled* and *struggled* to get free.

We can achieve a similar effect by listing:

eg He *huffed* and he *puffed* and he *blew* the house down.

A meaning can also be made more or less forceful by quantifying:

We saw *thousands* of seals.

There were *so many* problems to deal with.

Only a handful of people turned up.

… or in terms of extent:

It went on *for miles*. (place)

We *slept from midnight all the way through to late morning*. (time)

Various rhetorical strategies can be used to strengthen the interpersonal force in a text. By setting the tone towards the beginning, a context is established within which the rest of the text is interpreted, whether attitudes are stated explicitly or not.

■ identifying and analysing aspects of rhetoric in speeches drawn from contemporary and earlier contexts and students creating speeches of their own [Year 9]

Throughout the text, the interpersonal meanings tend to accumulate. Accumulation is often created through rhetorical patterns:

■ the repetition of key phrases (*Yes we can*)

- the use of parallelism, where the speaker/writer uses a refrain to create cohesion (*we shall fight on the beaches, we shall fight on the landing grounds, we shall fight in the fields and in the streets, we shall fight in the hills; we shall never surrender*)

- the 'rule of three',[10] where three instances or examples are provided to reinforce a point (*if all do their duty, if nothing is neglected, and if the best arrangements are made*).

- evaluating how speechmakers influence audiences through specific language features [Year 8]

Focus

We can use language to either sharpen or soften the focus of a message.

We sharpen the focus by narrowing the options:

eg It was a **genuine** mistake.

You're a **real** friend!

We soften the focus by broadening and blurring the options:

eg I was **kind of** relieved.

He did **sort of** a wild leap.

Opening up spaces

Perhaps the most common type of utterance is where we make a straightforward statement – no ambiguities, no multiple meanings, no attempt to entertain alternatives:

eg The government's refugee policy is flawed.

This is referred to as a 'bare assertion'. If we simply make bare assertions, there is little sensitivity to other possibilities and perspectives and interaction tends to be restricted to the level of either agreeing or disagreeing.

An alternative is to create spaces – for others to participate, for the consideration of alternative perspectives, values and possibilities. This has always been a highly valued aspect of English teaching, though we often don't look at how we do it through language.

Understand how to move beyond making bare assertions and take account of differing perspectives and points of view [Year 5]

Here we are concerned with engaging our listener/s or reader/s in various ways:

- inviting them to consider other perspectives

- introducing other voices into the discourse

- opening up (or closing down) spaces for negotiation

---

[10] Also referred to as a 'tricolon'.

■ entertaining other possibilities.

Most of what we say and write tends to be bare assertions, admitting only a single voice (the speaker or writer) or acknowledging only a single possibility. But overuse of such language has the effect of closing down interaction. Let's look at a range of resources for expanding (or contracting) the interaction and engaging with different voices, perspectives and possibilities.

■ recognising that a bare assertion (for example 'It's the best film this year') often needs to be tempered by: using the 'impersonal it' to distance oneself (for example 'It could be that it is the best film this year'); recruiting anonymous support (for example 'It is generally agreed that it is the best film this year.'); indicating a general source of the opinion (for example 'Most critics agree that it is the best film this year.'); specifying the source of the opinion (for example 'David and Margaret both agree that it is the best film this year.') and reflecting on the effect of these different choices [Year 5]

Attribution

One of the most obvious ways of introducing other voices and perspectives into the discourse is to explicitly refer to what others say or think about the topic under discussion. This can range from very vague references:

Some say ...

It is generally thought that ...

... through to the very specific:

In the words of Chairman Mao ...

McDonald (1997, 36) claims that ...

Understand conventions for citing others and how to reference these in different ways [Year 10]

Attribution can be found in a variety of registers, from casual conversation (*'But Daddy said that ...'*) through to serious written works. Students, for example, might want to look at how newspaper articles refer to sources of information, evaluating their credibility and status.

Feeling grumpy 'is good for you'

In a bad mood? Don't worry – **according to research**, it's good for you. An attack of the grumps can make you communicate better, **it is suggested.**

An Australian psychology expert who has been studying emotions has found being grumpy makes us think more clearly.

In contrast to those annoying happy types, miserable people are better at decision-making and less gullible, **his experiments showed.**

While cheerfulness fosters creativity, gloominess breeds attentiveness and careful thinking, **Professor Joe Forgas** told Australian Science Magazine.

The University of New South Wales researcher says a grumpy person

Mother: **Go** *to bed, Mick. It's late.*

[ten minutes later]

Mother: *You* **must** *be in bed in two minutes or else!*

Here we have Mother starting off with a rather 'weak' command (*you can go ...*). This is followed by a straight-out command (*go ...*) which then becomes more forceful (*you must ...*).

So here we have a continuum of 'obligation':

>   *must do* → *will do* → *might do*
>
>   *have to do* → *may do*
>
>   *have got to do* → *could do*

Again, we can express degrees of obligation through the use of modal adjuncts:

>   *You* **definitely** *have to come!*
>
>   *You might* **possibly** *like to come.*

And we also find expressions that have a modalising function (often using saying verbs):

>   *I suggest ...; I strongly recommend ...; You are required to ...; I order you to ...*
>   and *There is an expectation that ...*

The role of modality

Rather than simply making 'single-voiced' statements or issuing commands, modality allows us to open up or close down the space for negotiation. When we use low modality we encourage interaction by being somewhat tentative – using words like: *perhaps; maybe; we might like to ...; possibly; you could.* We can also use modality to contracting possibilities for negotiation by using words like *must, should* and *have to.*

Our use of modality depends on the context and, in particular, the tenor of the context, answering questions such as: Who has the status and authority to use high modality?; Who would use low modality?; In what circumstances?; To achieve what end? A person in an authoritarian role, for example, might give orders that are absolute ('must do'), whereas someone who wants to leave room for negotiation would choose low modality resources such as 'possibly', 'maybe', 'could', and 'might'. It is not always the case, however, that persons in authority will use high modality when getting someone to do something. Usually they realise the value of more subtle uses of modality. And similarly, those with a great deal of expertise will not necessarily use high modality in their statements. They generally recognise that few things can be stated categorically, and the more you know, the less likely you are to be adamant about the 'truth value' of a statement.

An awareness of how modality operates can make the difference between success and failure in our day-to-day interactions in various contexts. Job interviews can be lost, for example, through the misuse of modality. Essays can be marked down because students don't know how to temper their statements with the appropriate degree of commitment. Students who conclude an exposition with a highly 'modalised' blunt command, for example, (*'We **must** act now to save the environment!'*) will generally be marked lower than the student who can use high modality more indirectly (*'It is **imperative** that action be taken ...'*; *'It is **certain** that ...'*; *'Commonsense **dictates** that...'*) or who can employ lower modality, giving an impression of being aware of the validity of alternative positions (*'Most **would** agree that ...'*, *'While preserving the environment **could be** a high priority ...'*).

Modality is also a powerful resource for positioning people in particular ways. The ability to recognise how modality is being used by a writer, for example, can help the student become a critically aware reader. Students might, for example, analyse texts such as essays or textbooks to identify how low modality has been employed to introduce a note of circumspection or they might analyse advertisements in terms of their use of high and low modality (the 'hard sell' and the 'soft sell').

Contracting the interaction space

While there is merit in encouraging the listener/reader to engage freely with other possibilities, values and perspectives, there are times when we want to constrain that freedom and keep the listener/reader on a tighter leash. This is particularly the case when we are trying to persuade others to our point of view and want to maintain control of the argumentation.

Aligning with the listener/reader

When we engage in persuasive interaction, we generally seek to align ourselves with the values and interests of our audience. We try to imagine their expectations and to anticipate their response to what we are saying. In persuading someone to our point of view, we often make aligning moves. We can, for example, 'tell them what they want to hear'. This can be reinforced by expressions such as: *as you would be aware ...*; *we could agree that ...*; *of course*; *obviously* and *naturally*, which assume a shared knowledge and value system that can be taken for granted. (With a more resistant reader, however, such strategies might provoke a negative reaction.)

- identifying language that seeks to align the listener or reader (for example 'of course', 'obviously', 'as you can imagine') [Year 10]
- identifying references to shared assumptions [Year 10]
- identifying appeals to shared cultural knowledge, values and beliefs [Year 10]

In trying to influence the listener/reader, we might reinforce our position through such emphatic choices as: *the facts of the matter are ...*; *we can only conclude that ...*; *it is absolutely clear to me ...*, and *my firm belief is that ...*

Countering

If we are challenging a proposition, we might still acknowledge that there is more than one position, but then 'disalign' ourselves with it, using such expressions such as *'contrary to popular opinion ...'* or *'alternatively, we might consider ...'*.

When we are mounting an argument, it is strategic to anticipate the arguments that could be made against your position – but then to rebut them. Useful resources here are the contrastive and concessive conjunctions and connectives:

While we might agree that ...

Although there is an argument for ...

Even though we might concede that ...

However, it must be recognised that ...

On the other hand, ...

To no-one's surprise, he lost the match.

Amazingly he got away with it.

Negatives

In terms of meaning, the negative[13] often has the function of introducing an interpersonal tone involving contradiction, disapproval, opposition, denial, absence, and so on. This negative tenor is often found in text-types such as discussions and arguments:

*Birds should **not** be kept in cages.*
*One should **never** forget ...*

By using the negative, the speaker/writer is signalling that the positive is also in play, thereby opening up potential alternatives. In the following excerpt from a review, the use of the negative implies the alternative expectation that a compelling heroine **would** have dreams, motivations, ambitions, hopes, goals and original thoughts.

*Bella is a complete idiot. She has **no** dreams, **no** motivations, **no** ambitions, **no** hopes, **no** goals, and **not** a single original thought of her own.*

Having implicitly raised that possibility, however, the alternative is shut down by using the negative.

Negative expressions include:

no	not	none
nobody	nowhere	neither ... nor
nothing	no-one	not at all

Interacting with others: Monitoring student learning

Young learners

Young learners tend to be interpersonally unsophisticated and straightforward in their interactions. They will be very open in expressing their feelings and emotions and might make fairly basic evaluations of the qualities of things and of people's behaviour, based on their personal reactions. They will often state opinions in relation to their own experience without providing a rationale or evidence.

---

[13] Technically, the use of positive and negative expressions is referred to as 'polarity'.

- Are they given opportunities to extend the range of roles they take up in their school and community lives?

- Are they using a full range of questions, statements and commands to interact confidently with others?

- Are they becoming aware of group dynamics and how they can participate in whole-class, group and pair interactions in productive ways?

- In their discussions, writing and reading, are they noticing the different functions of statements, questions, commands and offers and how we use these? Are they able to form questions correctly – especially if they are ESL learners?

- In their writing, are they starting to be aware of the particular audience that they are writing for and how their language might change according to their reader?

Later primary

Students in later childhood are experimenting with more subtle and diverse ways of interacting, persuading and evaluating. Appraisal of qualities and judgements of behaviour tend to be fairly idiosyncratic, influenced by personal preferences and those of peers.

- Are students taking on a greater range of roles, both within the school context and the wider community?

- Are they comprehending and employing a wide variety of interaction resources in their oral language?

- Are they able to recognise different types of questions (eg yes/no, open, closed) and commands (eg direct and indirect) and see how these relate to the situation in which they are being used (eg in terms of status, power, authority, expertise, age) – who the questions are being asked by; what type of questions they are and who the commands are being given by and in what way?

- Can they reflect on the way in which interactions unfold and how they participate in terms of turn-taking and communication repairs?

- Are their interactions more extended and more sensitive to how different people are playing a role in the interaction?

- Are they sensitive to how the language used by their social groups can function to include or exclude others?

- Are they familiar with different terms of address, noticing how these function to establish certain kinds of relationships?

- Are they becoming more aware of the need to take the reader's expectations into account when writing and to seek to establish a relationship with the reader?

- Are opinions supported by evidence or a rationale?

- Are they learning to employ a greater range of modal resources?

- Do they recognise how the careful use of modality allows them to leave open spaces for other possibilities?

- Are they adjusting the degree of graduation rather than relying on strong pronouncements to persuade?

- Are they aware of the need to persuade through logic and evidence rather than emotion and strong statements of opinion?

- Can they identify ways in which they are being positioned through the language used by others?

Older learners

Older learners are developing much more flexible and confident control over interpersonal resources. They might enjoy exploring the notion of inter-textuality, including issues of creativity and originality. They could discuss how their own identities are formed through a myriad of intertextual encounters. They might reflect on the various discourse communities to which they belong and how solidarity is developed within these communities.

- Can they confidently adopt a wide range of roles in the school and broader community involving varying degrees of authority, expertise, and power – in small and large groups, with peers and teachers as well as unfamiliar persons?

- Are they able to reflect on the relationship between the roles they play in a range of contexts and the language resources, which are used in constructing those roles?

- Are they employing the resources of statements, questions, commands, offers and exclamations skilfully in developing successful interactions – initiating turns, making relevant contributions to maintaining and extending the topic, changing topic appropriately, supporting others, repairing communication breakdowns, and so on?

- Can they discuss the impact of using various types of questions, statements and commands in their interactions and how such speech functions can help to develop the characters in a narrative?

- Are they able to draw on an explicit knowledge about interpersonal resources to reflect on and discuss how the writer's attitude intrudes (eg through the use of comment adverbials) or when the writer emphasises or tones down a particular aspect of a statement (eg using force and focus), or when a writer uses high or low modality?

- In their discussions, writing, reading and viewing, are they able to critically analyse how certain types of language resources can be used to bias a text or influence the listener/speaker?

- Are they able to use modality more discerningly, recognising the need to allow for alternative points of view and other possibilities (using, for example, nominalisations such as 'likelihood' and 'necessity' rather than simply modal verbs such as 'might' and 'must')?

- Do they use graduation resources more subtly, including the use of 'downtoners' (eg *somewhat, rather*) to give an air of detachment.

- Rather than simply using strong intensifiers to persuade, can they employ other resources such as quantification and extent (*over several decades; throughout the world*) to give an appearance of objectivity?

- Are emotions nominalised when seeking to distance themselves (*Fear pervaded the room* vs. *we were afraid*)?

- Are their evaluations of the qualities of things (eg works of art, fashion, movies) grounded in criteria reflecting the values of the community rather than simply personal opinions?

- Are they making informed evaluations in terms of such factors as the aesthetic value of something, its composition, and its social significance?

- Are their judgements of human behaviour (eg the tragic hero) based on moral, ethical and legal considerations (eg capacity, endurance, social esteem, honesty)?

- Are their evaluations and judgements expressed both directly and indirectly (implied from the context)?

- Is the interpersonal tone of a text carefully managed, building up throughout the text?

- Do they consider the interests, values and expectations of their reader and do they use language in ways that will align or disalign with the audience?

- Can they problematise the notion of 'audience' – multiple audiences, unknown audiences, audiences with differing value systems, expert audiences, audiences with different agendas, expectations and purposes for reading?

- Are other voices and alternative perspectives introduced through both general and specific references to others' words and through intertextual allusions?

- As writers, are they aware of the conventions of citing and of the considerations involved in deciding whom to cite, why and how?

Interacting with others: analysed texts

The following two texts represent different blog responses to the novel *Gulliver's Travels* by Swift. From the interpersonal analysis, we can observe that the first review tends to centre on the reader's personal feelings reinforced by strong intensification (graduation), while the second focuses more on judging the capacity of the author, engaging with other perspectives, and evaluating the qualities of the text, drawing on a familiarity with cultural norms and values in literary appreciation rather than personal opinion.

TEXT A

Bare assertion
Exclamation
Expletive → Yuck. **What an awful book**. This was **probably** the **most boring,**

Setting
the tone
Engagement
(low modality)

-ve
Appreciation
High
Graduation
Engagement

repetitive, tedious book I have **EVER** had the displeasure of reading.

High
Graduation

Affect
(-ve emotion)

First person ("I") I thought this was **supposed to be** a classic. I **dragged myself** through

Affect (indirect
-ve emotion)

-ve
Appreciation
(indirect)

half this book and decided **life was too short to keep going. I heartily**

Affect (-ve
emotion)

dislike Jonathon Swift, but I can't help **feeling sorry** for him all

High
Graduation

the same.

Affect
(-ve emotion)

High
graduation

In the beginning, the stories were **so crushingly pointless** that I

-ve
Appreciation

Affect
(indirect
-ve emotion)

could barely keep reading. How many ridiculously named lands of

High
Graduation

oddly sized people can we **possibly** visit? **Keep reading** to find out!

-ve
Appreciation

Low
Graduation

At least the Yahoo 4th journey was **somewhat enjoyable. Probably**

Command
+ve
Appreciation

Affect (+ve
emotion)

because I **like** ponies.

Engagement
(low modality)

Affect (-ve
emotion)

I **don't care** if **it's considered** one of **the greatest satires ever written.**

Engagement
High
Graduation

For the most part I got a **complicated sentence structure that was**

+ve
Appreciation

tough to follow. **I had to put it down.** Literally. **If it was an animal,**

-ve
Appreciation

Affect
(indirect
-ve emotion)

I would have killed it and put it out of its misery. Pick up a copy

-ve
Appreciation
(indirect)

-ve
Appreciation

of Mein Kampf, because **ANYTHING** is more interesting than **this**

Command

-ve
Appreciation

insulting piece of drivel. Maybe next **I'll watch paint dry.** As my hand

-ve
Appreciation
(indirect)

Engagement
(low
modality)

reaches for another book off the classics shelf **I recoil in fear.**

Affect (-ve
emotion)

TEXT B

High graduation — Setting the tone

Swift's wildly fantastical, rude, scathing narrative is +ve Appreciation

High graduation

disturbingly relevant to contemporary geopolitics. Its **biting wit** +ve Appreciation

+ve Appreciation

and sarcastic examination of human nature are just as **interesting** as +ve Appreciation

High graduation

its **highly imaginative plot and characters**. Lemuel Gulliver's four trips +ve Appreciation

+ve Appreciation

to strange lands are **entertaining, humorous and trenchant**

Rhetorical question — Intertextuality

– what do you expect from the author of **"A Modest Proposal?"**

Focus +ve Appreciation

The fourth voyage **in particular** serves as **a searing indictment** of

First person pronoun -ve judgement of behaviour (abstractions)

what **we** now call **ethnocentrism, racism, economic imperialism,**

+ve Appreciation
High graduation **warmongering and piracy**.

High graduation

It is a **brilliant work**. There are **so many** levels of meaning that **can be**

+ve Judgement +ve Appreciation

explored. Swift is **great** because the satire arrives **so innocently, so**

+ve Appreciation
High graduation

lightly and so nonchalantly. His powers of description are **amazing**.

+ve Appreciation

The imagery and **precise** nature of the language employed by Swift

+ve Appreciation

brought the characters, people and surroundings to life.

Engagement (countering) +ve Appreciation

Swift's prose style is **surprisingly concise and direct**, considering

-ve Appreciation

the convoluted wordiness that one associates with the period. Like

Intertextuality +ve Judgement: capacity

Dickens, Swift is **adept** at mixing adventure with satire and giving

Engagement (countering)

things wonderful names that capture the feel of them. **Despite** his

High graduation +ve Appreciation

almost unbearable misanthropy (Mercy!), the book **succeeds** on the

+ve Appreciation

level of **pure, wondrous fantasy**.

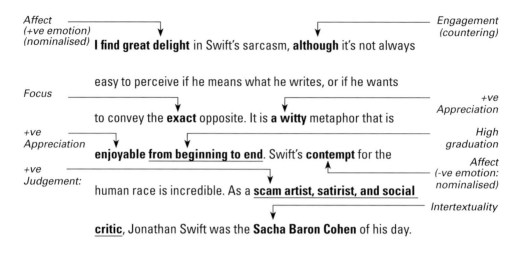

Affect (+ve emotion) (nominalised) **I find great delight** in Swift's sarcasm, **although** it's not always *Engagement (countering)*

easy to perceive if he means what he writes, or if he wants

Focus to convey the **exact** opposite. It is **a witty** metaphor that is *+ve Appreciation*

+ve Appreciation **enjoyable from beginning to end**. Swift's **contempt** for the *High graduation*

+ve Judgement: human race is incredible. As a **scam artist, satirist, and social** *Affect (-ve emotion: nominalised)*

Intertextuality

critic, Jonathan Swift was the **Sacha Baron Cohen** of his day.

The final paragraph illustrates the need to interpret a text within its context. In mainstream culture, for example, being sarcastic, having contempt for the human race and being a scam artist would be negatively valued. Here, however, the reviewer is subverting those values, perhaps aligning with a youthful discourse community that delights in going against the grain.

5 Creating cohesive texts

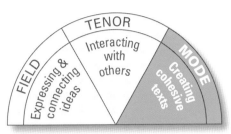

So far, we have looked at how language functions to represent and connect ideas and to enable interaction. A further function of language is to shape texts in a way that is cohesive and coherent. The ways in which texts are shaped, however, depends on the mode – or 'channel of communication' – being used: spoken, written, or visual. In this chapter we will focus primarily on the construction of carefully crafted written texts.

> Understand that some language of written texts is unlike everyday spoken language [Foundation]

Organising the flow of information

One of the challenges facing readers is how to recognise the overall structuring of the text. For the writer, the challenge is to organise the text in a way that makes the meaning accessible to the reader. When students start to create longer texts, many find it difficult to manage the flow of information through the text. Here we will look at how coherence can be achieved at the level of the text, the paragraph and the sentence.

Text level organisation

Many (but not all) texts announce to the reader how the text will unfold. This prepares the reader to anticipate a certain way that the content will be organised in the text. We could call this the 'text opener' – how the beginning of the text helps the reader to predict what is to come.

> Understand that the coherence of more complex texts relies on devices that signal text structure and guide readers, for example overviews, initial and concluding paragraphs and topic sentences, indexes or site maps, or breadcrumb trails for online texts [Year 7]

In the following text by Guy Talese, for example, the text opener[1] prepares the reader to expect a certain line of argumentation:

> **New York is a city of things unnoticed.** It is a city with cats sleeping under parked cars, two stone armadillos crawling up St Patrick's Cathedral, and thousands of ants creeping on top of the Empire State Building ...

---

[1] This is sometimes called the Macrotheme.

Here we have the theme revealed in the first line. It becomes the 'controlling idea' for the rest of the text: that New York is populated by anonymous, shadowy yet fascinating beings.

Some texts refrain from telling the reader how the text will develop. Others might do so after some preliminary background information.

Paragraph level organisation

One thing that adds to the coherence of a text is the way we divide it into paragraphs. The author needs to decide how to divide the written material into manageable and logical 'bundles', each of which deals with a single, unified topic or event. The length of a paragraph can range from an individual sentence through to a considerable number of sentences. Paragraphs help the reader to discern the major points being made in the text and the shifts between those points.

Understand that paragraphs are a key organisational feature of written texts [Year 3]

A paragraph generally contains a 'paragraph opener' or topic sentence.[2] This typically occurs at the beginning of the paragraph and announces the main point being made in the paragraph. It is often a relatively general statement, which is followed up in the rest of the paragraph with various elaborations such as examples, definitions, description, supporting evidence, and so on – depending on the purpose of the text.

■ noticing how longer texts are organised into paragraphs, each beginning with a topic sentence/paragraph opener which predicts how the paragraph will develop and is then elaborated in various ways [Year 3]

In the New York text, for example, each paragraph expands on the theme of 'things unnoticed'. These 'sub-themes' are flagged in the topic sentence:

1 **Some of New York's best informed men are elevator operators who rarely talk but always listen – like doormen.** Sardi's doormen listen to the comments made by Broadway's first-nighters walking by after the last act. They listen closely. They listen carefully. They can tell you within ten minutes which shows will flop and which will be hits. ...

2 **New York is a town of 3,000 bootblacks whose brushes and rhythmic rag-snaps can be heard up and down Manhattan from midmorning to midnight.** They dodge cops, survive rainstorms, and thrive in the Empire State Building as well as on the Staten Island Ferry. They usually wear dirty shoes. ...

3 **When street traffic dwindles and most people are sleeping, some New York neighbourhoods begin to crawl with cats.** They move quickly through the shadows of buildings. ...

4 **In every New York neighbourhood, the strays are dominated by a 'boss' – the largest, strongest tomcat.** But, except for the boss, there

---

[2]   This is sometimes called the Hypertheme.

is not much organisation in the street cat's society. Within the society, however, there are three 'types' of cats – wild cats, Bohemians, and part-time grocery store (or restaurant) cats.

- Paragraph 1 begins with the topic sentence – *Some of New York's best informed men are elevator operators, who rarely talk, but always listen – like doormen.* – which is elaborated on with an example of how Sardi's doormen (another of New York's 'unnoticed') listen silently but intently to the first-nighters.

- The topic sentence of Paragraph 2 – *New York is a town of 3,000 bootblacks whose brushes and rhythmic rag-snaps can be heard up and down Manhattan from midmorning to midnight* – introduces another of New York's silent inhabitants, the bootblacks, who are then described in the ensuing sentences.

- Several paragraphs then take up the theme of New York cats, and with each topic sentence flagging different aspects of the cats' lives in the city.

Understand how cohesion in texts is improved by strengthening the internal structure of paragraphs through the use of examples, quotations and substantiation of claims [Year 8]

The beginning of the paragraph does the job of linking back to the overarching theme of the text as well as providing the basis for the development of the paragraph. The end of the paragraph can also perform a couple of different jobs – sometimes bringing home the point of the paragraph, sometimes foreshadowing how the following text will unfold.

Sentence level organisation

At the sentence level, the flow of information in the text is controlled by the choice of 'sentence opener' or Theme. The technical term 'Theme' refers to the beginning of the clause. The beginnings of the clauses focus our attention on how the topic is being developed. This helps to make the text coherent at the 'micro' level and to enable the reader to follow how the text is unfolding.

Understand that the starting point of a sentence gives prominence to the message in the text and allows for prediction for how the text will unfold [Year 5]

> **Some of New York's best informed men** are elevator operators who rarely talk but always listen – like doormen.
> **Sardi's doormen** listen to the comments made by Broadway's first-nighters walking by after the last act.
>
> **They** listen closely.
> **They** listen carefully.
> **They** can tell you within ten minutes which shows will flop and which will be hits. ...

- observing how writers use the beginning of a sentence to signal to the reader how the text is developing (for example 'Snakes are reptiles. They have scales and no legs. Many snakes are poisonous. However, in Australia they are protected') [Year 5]

The beginning of each sentence (or Theme – in bold in the above text) alerts us to the topic that is being developed. In the paragraph above, the Theme is **Some of New York's best informed men**, which becomes more specific (**Sardi's doormen**), which is then picked up as **they**.

Theme ('topic')	New information
1 **Some of New York's best informed men**	*are elevator operators who rarely talk but always listen – like doormen.*
2 **Sardi's doormen**	*listen to the comments made by Broadway's first-nighters walking by after the last act.*
3 **They**	*listen closely.*
4 **They**	*listen carefully.*
5 **They**	*can tell you within ten minutes which shows will flop and which will be hits.*

While the beginning of the sentence (or the clause) primarily focuses our attention on how the topic of the text is developing, the end of the sentence tends to introduce new information about the topic. Notice how, in Sentence 2, new information is introduced (*like doormen*), which is then taken up in the next sentence as its Theme, *Sardi's doormen*, which then continues as Theme for the next few sentences.

Similarly, the end of Paragraph 4 signals the development of the next few paragraphs:

... Within the society, however, there are three 'types' of cats	*– wild cats, Bohemians, and part-time grocery store (or restaurant) cats.*
The wild cats	*rely on an occasional loose garbage bin lid or on rats for food ...*
The Bohemian,	*however, is more tractable. It does not run from people. ...*
The part-time grocery store (or restaurant) cat,	*often a reformed Bohemian, eats well and keeps rodents away. ...*

Another Theme that is layered over the New York text is that of time. The various 'things unnoticed' appear at different times of the day and night, and we are guided through a typical day:

At Broadway in the evening, a big, dark 1948 Rolls Royce pulls in ...

By this time, Fifth Avenue is deserted by all but a few strolling insomniacs ...

When street traffic dwindles and most people are sleeping, some New York neighbourhoods begin to swarm with cats.

> **At 5 a.m.** Manhatten is a town of tired trumpet players and homeward-bound bartenders.
>
> **At 5 a.m.** the Broadway regulars have gone home or to all-night coffee shops ...
>
> **At 6 a.m.** the early workers begin to push up from the subways.

The careful choice of Theme adds to the predictability of texts, making them easier to read. It is often useful to familiarise students with the need to focus on the beginning of the clause to get an idea of the 'theme' and on the end for the new information.

There are a number of possible Theme patterns which a writer can draw upon in writing a text:

- in a recount the writer might use the beginning of the clause to develop the timeline, eg, *In 1968 ...*; *Later on ...*; *In the early 70s ...*; *Soon after ...*

- in a procedure the beginning focus is generally on the sequence of actions which need to be carried out, eg, *Pour ...* ; *Mix ...* ; *Stir ...* ; *Bake ...*

- in an exposition, the beginning of the clause is often used to structure the argument, eg, *Firstly ...*; *However ...*; *In conclusion ...* .

Sometimes, particularly in literary texts such as narratives and poems, the writer might want to unsettle the reader or to highlight the unusual. This often involves making an unexpected choice of Theme.[3]

> **Slobbering and foolish**, the young retriever dog jumped excitedly all over them.
>
> **Stimulated by the crisis**, Andy's brain began to work.
>
> **Less measurable but no less profound** is a sapping of confidence across our land (Barack Obama – inaugural speech).
>
> **Down** came a jumbuck to drink at the water-hole,
> **Up** jumped the swagman and grabbed him with glee.

- recognising how emphasis in sentences can be changed by re-ordering clauses [Year 10]

These are stylistic decisions that the author has made in order to arouse interest and focus on a particular aspect. Young writers might be encouraged to find examples of such uses and to reflect on the effect of making different choices in Theme position.

TROUBLESHOOTING

It is careful attention to Theme that makes a text more coherent and considerate towards the reader. The Theme signals to the reader: 'This is what I want you to pay attention to' ...; 'Now I'm shifting my focus' ...; 'Now I want you to attend to this' ...; 'Now I'm introducing another aspect of the theme' ... and so on.

---

[3] Technically, this is referred to as 'marked Theme'.

Text connectives

Other words that contribute to the cohesion of the text are the text connectives. These are often referred to using terms such as 'connectors', 'discourse markers' or 'signal words'. They provide the reader with signposts indicating how the text is developing and linking stretches of text. If the writer wants to show that a summary is coming up, for example, a phrase such as *In short* ... or *Briefly* ... can be used. If the text is giving a sequence of points, these can be highlighted by the use of such words as: *To begin* ...; *Secondly* ...; *In conclusion*... .

■ describing how texts connectives link sections of a text providing sequences through time, for example 'firstly', 'then', 'next', and 'finally' [Year 4]

The following is a list of commonly used text connectives.

Clarifying	Showing cause/result	Indicating time
in other words	therefore	then
I mean	then	next
to put it another way	consequently	afterwards
for example	as a consequence	at the same time
for instance	as a result	before that
to be more precise	for that reason	in the end
or rather	accordingly	finally
in particular	because of this	after a while
in fact	in that case	at this point
as a matter of fact		meanwhile
that is		at this moment
namely		later
to illustrate		previously
		earlier
		until then

Sequencing ideas	Adding information	Condition/concession/contrast
firstly, first	in addition	in that case
in the first place	apart from that	otherwise
first of all	too	if not
to start with	furthermore	however
to begin	also	nevertheless
for a start	on top of that	on the contrary
second, third, fourth	and besides	despite this
at this point	above all	besides
to get back to the point	along with	on the other hand
in short	what's more	anyhow, anyway
all in all	again	instead
briefly	as well	still
to summarise/to sum up	likewise	even so
finally	moreover	all the same
a final point	similarly	in any case
to conclude	equally	at least
in conclusion	in the same way	though
given the above points		
in light of the above		

TROUBLESHOOTING

Sometimes text connectives are confused with conjunctions, and indeed they often perform a very similar function. Conjunctions, however, join two clauses and only operate within a sentence. Text connectives, on the other hand, form links between sentences and other longer stretches of text. Also, while conjunctions are placed at the beginning of a clause, text connectives can be more freely placed at various positions within the sentence (as, for example, in the use of *however* and *on the other hand* in this paragraph).

Deletions and substitutions

Rather than repeating a word, we often simply delete the repetition.[6] This creates a link as the reader is forced to think back to what word the deletion refers.

- noting how writers often leave out words that have already been mentioned (for example 'Tina ate three apples and Simon ate two [apples]') [Year 6]

---

[6] This is referred to technically as 'ellipsis'.

'Kokou must be hungry.'

But he was not ~~hungry~~.

She was short and dumpy and ~~she~~ had one leg a bit shorter than the other ~~leg~~.

If she wasn't around, I'd be doing something interesting right now. ~~If she wasn't around,~~ I'd be climbing Mount Kilimanjaro. ~~If she wasn't around,~~ I'd be starring in the latest Hollywood blockbuster.

Alice was beginning to get very tired of sitting by her sister on the bank, and ~~Alice was beginning to get very tired~~ of having nothing to do.

Understand that cohesive links can be made in texts by omitting or replacing words [Year 6]

We can also create a link in a text by using 'all-purpose' words that replace[7] verb groups or noun groups or even whole clauses (eg *do, so, such, one*):

Replacing a verb: '*I told him to leave*. And he **did**.'

Replacing a noun: *I've two umbrellas. Would you like* **one**?

Replacing a clause: *She was very tired*. Yes, I thought **so**.

- noting how writers often substitute a general word for a more specific word already mentioned, thus creating a cohesive link between the words (for example 'Look at those apples. Can I have one?') [Year 6]

Such strategies reduce repetition, redundancy and clumsiness in texts.

TROUBLESHOOTING

Ellipsis ('leaving words out') and substitution (replacing words with other 'all-purpose' words) can cause problems for some younger readers and those having difficulties with fluency. In particular, ESL learners often find such deletions and substitutions mystifying, and might need some intensive work in this area.

Word associations

Compare and contrast the use of cohesive devices in texts, focusing on how they serve to signpost ideas, to make connections, to build semantic associations between ideas [Year 9]

Another way in which links are set up within a text is through word associations,[8] eg:

- repetition
- synonyms
- antonyms
- collocation
- word patterns (class/subclass; part/whole; activity sequence).

---

[7] This is referred to technically as 'substitution'.
[8] This is referred to technically as 'lexical cohesion' – or cohesion between content words/lexical items.

Understand how coherence is created in complex texts through devices like lexical cohesion, ellipsis, grammatical theme and text connectives. [Year 8]

Repetition

In the text on page 151, certain words (eg *Jackdaw*) are repeated. This is the most simple kind of cohesion, where we can easily track the Participants because they are referred to using the same word through the text. Another type of repetition is often used for rhetorical purposes, where a refrain keeps occurring.

- recognising how cohesion can be developed through repeating key words or by using synonyms or antonyms [Year 6]

> The scene was a plain, bare, monotonous vault of a schoolroom, and the speaker's square forefinger emphasised his observations by underscoring every sentence with a line on the schoolmaster's sleeve. **The emphasis was helped** by the speaker's square wall of a forehead, which had his eyebrows for its base, while his eyes found commodious cellarage in two dark caves, overshadowed by the wall. **The emphasis was helped** by the speaker's mouth, which was wide, thin, and hard set. **The emphasis was helped** by the speaker's voice, which was inflexible, dry, and dictatorial. **The emphasis was helped** by the speaker's hair, which bristled on the skirts of his bald head, a plantation of firs to keep the wind from its shining surface, all covered with knobs, like the crust of a plum pie, as if the head had scarcely warehouse-room for the hard facts stored inside.
>
> *Hard Times*, C. Dickens

Understand patterns of repetition and contrast in simple texts [Year 1]

This is referred to as 'parallelism' and creates a cohesive pattern in the text.

Synonyms

Another way of forming a 'lexical' link is to use 'synonyms' (ie words which have a similar meaning). In the text on page 151, the Jackdaw is also referred to as *the intruder*, while the Peacocks are called *those beautiful birds* and *his betters*. The birds' plumage is also referred to as *feathers* and *plumes*. On the one hand, this adds interest and subtlety to the text, but on the other hand it can make it difficult for inexperienced readers and ESL students to track the Participants.

Understand how texts are made cohesive through resources, for example word associations, synonyms, and antonyms [Year 2]

Antonyms

Similarly, 'antonyms' can be used to create a different type of link. Antonyms are opposite in meaning rather than similar. In the Jackdaw text, for example, we find *his drab plumage* contrasted with *the brilliant colours* of the Peacocks. There is also the contrast between *a vain Jackdaw* and *the humbled Jackdaw*.

Collocation

'Collocation' is a term used for words that typically occur together, making a text predictable. In the text about the Jackdaw, for example, we find *river, bank, water* and *reflection*.

> **A dark leaden-coloured mass** is creeping over **the sky** towards **the sun**. Red zigzags of **lightning** gleam here and there across it. There is a sound of **far-away rumbling. A warm wind** frolics over the grass, bends the trees, and stirs up the dust. In a minute there will be **a spurt of May rain** and **a real storm** will begin.
>
> *A Day in the Country*
> Anton Chekhov

sky

leaden-coloured mass

sun

storm

lightning

rain

wind

- mapping examples of word associations in texts, for example words that refer to the main character [Year 2]

Word patterns

- identifying patterns of vocabulary items in texts (for example class/subclass patterns, part/whole patterns, compare/contrast patterns, cause-and-effect patterns, word associations/collocation) [Year 1]

Word patterns are particular 'clusters' of words in a text that are related in various ways. They might, for example, be related in terms of 'class' and 'subclass'.

> Camels are humped, long-necked mammals of **the genus *Camelus*** that live in the dry desert areas.
>
> There are **two types** of camels: the **dromedary** or Arabian camel which has a single hump and the **Bactrian** camel which are two humps and come from central eastern Asia. The Bactrian is shorter than the Dromedary and has longer, finer wool.
>
> There are six camel-like creatures in **the family Camelidae**: the two **true camels**, and the four South American **camelids**, the llama, alpaca, guanaco, and vicuña.

- observing how relationships between concepts can be represented visually through similarity, contrast, juxtaposition, repetition, class-subclass diagrams, part-whole diagrams, cause-and-effect figures, visual continuities and discontinuities [Year 6]

This pattern could be represented as a classification taxonomy:

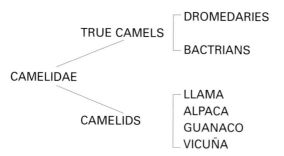

- observing how concepts, information and relationships can be represented visually through such images as tables, maps, graphs, diagrams, and icons [Year 6]

Or they might be related in terms of 'whole' and 'part', such as the body parts of the camel.

> A camel's thick **coat** reflects sunlight, and also insulates them from the intense heat from desert sand. Their long **legs** help by keeping them further from the hot ground. Their **mouth** is very sturdy, able to chew thorny desert plants. Long **eyelashes** and **ear hairs**, together with sealable **nostrils**, keep the sand the dust out and a **third eyelid** acts as a windshield wiper, moving from side to side to wipe the sand away. Even though their **ears** are quite small, they have excellent hearing. Their wide **feet** spread out so they won't sink in the sand.

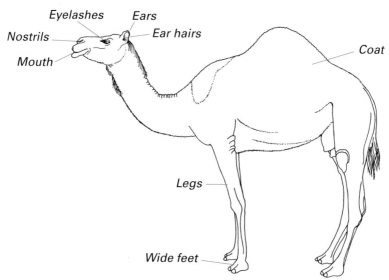

TROUBLESHOOTING

Students often need support in recognising patterns such as 'class-subclass' and 'part-whole'. Guiding students to identify such patterns and representing them as in the above diagrams forces the learner to read the text carefully and purposefully.

In sequential texts such as recounts, stories, explanations and procedures, the pattern will be more of an 'action sequence', identified by a succession of processes.

> When the sun **heats** the oceans, liquid water from the ocean's surface *evaporates* into water vapour in the air. The sun **heats** this air (water vapour and all) so that it **rises** through the atmosphere and **is carried** along by wind currents. As this water vapour **rises**, it **cools down** again, *condensing* into droplets of liquid water (or crystals of solid ice). Some of this water **collects** in large, underground reservoirs, but most of it **forms** rivers and streams that **flow** into the oceans.[9]

1 The sun heats the ocean.
2 Ocean water evaporates and rises into the air.
3 The water vapour cools and condenses to become droplets, which form clouds.

4 If enough water condenses, the drops become heavy enough to fall to the ground as rain and snow.
5 Some rain collects in ground wells. The rest flows through rivers back into the ocean.

- observing how sequential events can be represented visually by a series of images, including comic strips, timelines, photo stories, procedure diagrams and flowcharts, life-cycle diagrams, and the flow of images in picture books [Year 6]

Word chains

If we want to trace the main participants in a text, we can draw up 'word chains' by noting the various ways in which they are referred to in the text.

the Jackdaw	his companions	the Peacocks
a vain Jackdaw	his old companions	the brilliant colours
drab plumage	his former companions	the Peacock
his reflection	his old flock	feathers
the intruder	their society	the Peacocks
his borrowed plumes	his equals	a flock
the humbled Jackdaw		those beautiful birds
		beaks
		claws
		his betters

- identifying how a topic is described throughout a text by tracking noun groups and pronouns [Year 4]

---

[9] http://science.howstuffworks.com/nature/natural-disasters/flood1.htm

All the cohesive devices above set up different types of links in the text, weaving a tapestry of meaning for the reader to perceive and appreciate. Students need to be able to create these patterns in their own writing with increasing sophistication and need to be able to interpret the cohesive links when reading texts – a skill not fully developed until adulthood.

Features of mature written texts

As students move into secondary school, they will encounter and create texts that are characteristic of the kinds of written texts that require careful crafting and reflection. Such texts are typically quite dense and contain high levels of nominalisation and abstraction. This becomes clear when we look at the following text.

Human impact on aquatic ecosystems

All ecosystems are having to deal with the problem of human impact on an unprecedented scale. Aquatic ecosystems are being increasingly damaged because human beings are intervening irresponsibly in the natural environment.

The main factors affecting these ecosystems include the inappropriate disposal of rubbish, nutrient or sediment run off, habitat destruction and fragmentation, and depletion of local species through overfishing.

Contamination of the natural environment through inappropriate disposal of rubbish and a range of pollutants – herbicides, pesticides, fertilisers, industrial effluents, and human waste products – is one of the most pernicious contemporary issues confronting the environment.

Habitat destruction and fragmentation disrupts ecological processes so that remaining ...

Density

Let's take a sentence from the text: *Aquatic ecosystems are being increasingly damaged because human beings are intervening irresponsibly in the natural environment.*

This is obviously a sentence from a very 'written' text. If we wanted to make it accessible for a young person we would probably make it sound more 'spoken':

> *"Certain animals and plants live in the water and they interact with each other and form communities and these communities also interact with other non-living things. And this is called an ecosystem. But these ecosystems are being damaged because human beings keep butting in and mucking up the environment."*

Notice that in the spoken version we have taken eight clauses to get the message across. Each of those clauses contains only a small number of content words (lexical items: nouns; verbs; adverbs and adjectives). In the rapid flow of spoken language, we can't cope with a lot of content all at once, so we space it out. Typically, we use between two and four lexical items per clause:

1 *Certain **animals** and **plants live** in the **water*** [4]

2 *and they **interact** with each other* [1]

3 *and they **form communities*** [2]

4 *and these **communities** also **interact** with other **non-living things*** [4]

5 *and this is **called** an **ecosystem*** [2]

6 *but these **ecosystems** are being **damaged*** [2]

7 *because **human beings** keep **butting in*** [3]

8 *and **mucking up** the **environment**.* [2]

In the 'written' version, only two clauses have been used to represent virtually the same information, with somewhat more lexical items per clause, increasing the density.

1 ***Aquatic ecosystems** are being **increasingly damaged*** [4]

2 *because **human beings** are **intervening irresponsibly** in the **natural environment**.* [6]

We could reduce the same information to a single clause, resulting in a very 'written' sentence containing ten lexical items:

1 *The **result** of **irresponsible human intervention** in the **natural environment** is **increasing degradation** of **aquatic ecosystems**.* [10]

The sentence has now become very lexically dense – typical of adult written texts.

TROUBLESHOOTING

As students move from primary school and through the secondary school, texts become increasingly dense. This is an aspect of literacy that students haven't encountered previously. The ability to read and write such texts can't be taken for granted and needs to be dealt with explicitly.

Nominalisation

If we look at the last sentence above, we can see how the language has been compacted in the shift from spoken to written. Most of the compacting has been brought about by a shift towards noun groups (nominalisation).

> Understand the effect of nominalisation in the writing of informative and persuasive texts [Year 8]

The notion of causality, previously expressed in the conjunction *because* joining two clauses, has now been nominalised into a 'thing': *the result*. What were activities (*'human beings keep butting in and mucking up the environment'*) have now become 'things' represented by dense noun groups (*irresponsible human intervention in the natural environment* and *increasing degradation of aquatic ecosystems*). In the process of nominalisation, whole clauses are collapsed into noun groups. Other examples from the text include:

human impact

contamination of the natural environment

the inappropriate disposal of rubbish

habitat destruction and fragmentation

depletion of local species through overfishing.

■ analysing formal and persuasive texts to identify and explain language choices such as nominalisation [Year 8]

TROUBLESHOOTING

On the one hand, nominalisation can be a useful strategy for compacting information and making texts tighter. The texts of students who can use it effectively tend to be more highly evaluated. On the other hand, it has the effect of making texts very dense and difficult to read. Students need support in 'unpacking' nominalisation back to the 'spoken' form of clauses, eg:

habitat destruction and fragmentation

→　　　"people are destroying the habitat of the creatures

　　　and they are fragmenting the places where they live"

Abstraction

Mature writing in educational contexts tends to contain a great deal of abstraction. Some abstract terms serve the function of summarising a whole concept. The word 'ecosystem' for example is a summing up of:

1 *Certain animals and plants live in the water*

2 *and they interact with each other*

3 *and they form communities*

4 *and these communities also interact with other non-living things*

5 *and this is called an **ecosystem**.*

■ Exploring sections of academic and technical texts and analysing the use of abstract nouns to compact and distil information, structure argument and summarise preceding explanations [Year 9]

Abstract words like 'problem' and 'issue' assume an understanding of all the things that constitute the problem or issue. '*The problem of human impact*', for example, summarises the rest of the text, which is an elaboration of what the problem is. Other examples from the text include:

*the main **factors** affecting these ecosystems*

*one of the most pernicious contemporary **issues***

*ecological **processes**.*

Abstractions of this kind are essential in writing mature arguments, where they function to summarise stretches of the argument:

issue	purpose	evidence	factor
point	topic	approach	perspectives
debate	criticism	account	argument
idea	strategy	opinion	knowledge
thesis	view	statement	report
claim	assertion	proposition	question
dispute	debate	thought	belief
notion	discovery	assumption	

Understand how certain abstract nouns can be used to summarise preceding or subsequent stretches of text [Year 9]

Such abstractions can serve either to summarise:

> Images of hunger and pain allow us to meditate upon the implications of such hunger and pain – namely, the feelings of helplessness, of being abandoned, alone, of having no control, of losing the structure we know to be ourselves. Doing this, we are actually dealing with our present predicament,

because these are the **issues** that often arise in our daily lives.

… or to foreshadow:

A **problem** had arisen at work

> – an awkward matter which was the reason I'd phoned his wife yesterday. I'd opened the mail the other day and in an envelope with a South African stamp I'd found a photocopy of a clipping from what seemed like some local African newspaper, dated June 1997. That would have been when Jarawa was already at the UN. The article reported that Jarawa had separated from his wife. It also mentioned rumours that she had shown up one night at a hospital at two in the morning with a cracked rib and covered in bruises.[10] etc.

TROUBLESHOOTING

The shift into abstraction is a major challenge for students who are used to dealing with concrete, physical experiences. It is often useful to monitor their understanding of such abstractions during reading ('What is the issue?'; 'What is *proposition* referring to?') and to model the use of abstractions to support their writing ('Look how the author has predicted what will be coming: *There are many factors contributing to this problem.*').

---

[10] Wilcken, H. (2001) *The Execution*, Harper-Collins

Creating cohesive texts: Monitoring student learning

Young learners

- Can young students structure a simple oral text coherently (eg recounting in chronological order the events of the previous day; telling someone how to carry out a procedure in sequential steps)?

- Can they write brief, well-structured texts that do not assume a shared knowledge?

- Can they identify paragraph breaks and discuss the reason for paragraphs?

- When writing longer texts, can they demonstrate an awareness of the need to use paragraphs?

- Are they starting to move beyond writing that has the features of spoken language (eg lacking the explicit, tight cohesion and text organisation typical of written language)?

- In reading, can they track the main participants in a text through the use of pronouns and other referring words?

- Can they discuss in broad, basic terms how a simple, familiar text has been organised?

Later primary

- Can students structure a wider range of oral and written texts in a coherent and cohesive manner?

- Can they discuss how they have organised their texts in ways that are sensitive to the needs of the reader?

- Can students use paragraphs to organise the subject matter of their written texts?

- Are they starting to use topic sentences, Theme and text connectives effectively?

- Can they identify some of the cohesive features that are characteristic of a particular text type? In relation to text connectives, for example, argument or discussion might employ connectives such as *firstly, on the one hand,* and *in conclusion.* An explanation might include connectives that indicate causality and condition, such as *therefore* or *consequently.* A recount will typically use text connectives that help to sequence the events, such as *then, afterwards* and *eventually.*

- Can they discuss the links in a text created by basic cohesive devices (eg pronouns referring back to a noun group) using appropriate terminology?

- Do their written texts display a greater control over cohesive devices (eg referring words and word associations), sounding less like spoken language?

- In their reading, do they comprehend fluently, tracking the meaning as it develops through the text?

- Are they drawing on a range of cohesive devices to make inferences?

- Can they identify the relationships between content words in a text (eg words with a similar meaning, words with an opposite meaning, words which often occur together, words which form a meaningful pattern)? In an information report, for example, can they find nouns related in terms of a hierarchy (class-subclass), or in terms of part-whole relationships, or in terms of similarities or differences. In a story, can they recognise relationships developed through collocation and sequences of activities?

Older learners

- Are they able to reflect on and discuss the ways in which texts can be structured in predictable ways – but also how to play with predictability to achieve particular effects, particularly in literary texts?

- Can they identify text openers, paragraph openers and sentence openers and discuss their function?

- Are students reading lengthy texts, navigating their way using text openers, paragraph openers, and sentence openers as well as headings, subheadings and other textual organisers such as connectives?

- Are they familiar with a range of different text connectives and the role they play in structuring a text?

- Are they using terms such as 'synonym', 'antonym' and 'collocation' to refer to how words and ideas are related?

- Are they able to recognise various patterns in texts such as class-subclass and part-whole?

- Can they readily infer meaning, drawing on strategies involving substitution, ellipsis, referring words, word associations, synonyms and antonyms?

- Are they writing extended texts that guide the reader through the text and that have the characteristic language features of tightly-organised, carefully crafted, compact written texts, with thought given to paragraphing, topic sentences, Theme choices and text connectives?

- Are they able to identify nominalisations and abstractions and to notice how these generally function to make texts more compact by condensing whole clauses (nominalisation) or whole concepts (abstraction)?

- Are they able to understand and purposefully use nominalisations and abstractions in academic writing?

Creating cohesive texts: Analysed text

Instances of ellipsis (leaving words out, forcing the reader to infer them from the previous text) are indicated by inserting the omitted words and then placing them in blue/strike through, ~~like this~~. Reference items are in *italics* and the items they are referring back to are <u>underlined</u>. Text connectives are **in bold**.

<u>Alice</u> found herself in a long, low hall, which was lit up by a row

of lamps hanging from the roof. Suddenly *she* came upon

pronoun

a little three-legged <u>table</u>, all made of solid glass. There was

pronoun

nothing on *it* except a tiny <u>golden key</u>. *She* took *the* little golden

pronoun;
article

article

key from *the* <u>glass table</u>, and ~~she~~ unlocked the door that led into a

beautiful garden. A large <u>rose-tree</u> stood near the entrance of *the*

article

pronoun

garden. The <u>roses</u> growing on *it* were white, but there were

pronoun

three <u>gardeners</u> at *it*, busily painting *them* red. Alice thought *this*

pronoun;
demonstrative

a very curious thing.

pronoun;

'Would *you* tell *me*,' *she* asked, a little timidly, 'why *you* are

pronoun;
pronoun;
demonstrative

painting *those* roses?' …

pronoun;
pronoun

At this moment Five, who had been anxiously looking across the

garden, called out 'The Queen! The Queen!' and <u>the three</u>

<u>gardeners</u> instantly threw themselves flat upon *their* faces.

First came ten soldiers carrying clubs. **Next** ~~came~~ <u>the ten courtiers</u>;

substitution
(demonstrative)

these were ornamented all over with diamonds, and ~~they~~ <u>walked two</u>

substitution;
substitution
(demonstrative)

<u>and two</u>, as the soldiers *did*. After *these* came the royal children,

walking *in similar fashion*. **Then** came the <u>guests</u>, mostly Kings and

comparative

Queens, and among *them* <u>Alice</u> recognised <u>the White Rabbit</u>. *It* was

pronoun

pronoun

talking in a hurried nervous manner and ~~it~~ went by without noticing *her*.

And, last of all in *this* grand procession, came THE KING AND QUEEN   *demonstrative*

2 LANGUAGE FOR CONNECTING IDEAS

Clauses can be combined to represent the logical relationships between ideas.

PROBE QUESTION	FUNCTION	REALISED TYPICALLY BY THE GRAMMATICAL CLASS OF:	EXAMPLE
'How can we combine these ideas?'	**expanding**		
	– linking bits of information	**group + group**	*very loud **and** clear* *tired **but** happy* *for a minute **or** two*
	– coordination (linking messages of equal status in terms of eg addition, contrast, cause)	**independent clause + independent clause/s** (compound sentence) joined by **coordinating conjunctions** (eg and, but, so, yet, or, neither… nor)	*They all moved off, // **and** Alice was soon left alone.* *This sounded nonsense, // **but** Alice very obediently got up.* *Alice didn't want to begin another argument. // **so** she said nothing.* *Your hair has become very white; // **yet** you incessantly stand on your head.*
	– subordination (binding together messages of unequal status in terms of eg time, reason, condition, concession)	■ **independent clause + dependent clause/s** (complex sentence) joined by **subordinating conjunctions** (eg when, until, because, if, although)	***When** Alice looked up,// there was nothing to be seen.* *Why did you call him Tortoise // **if** he wasn't one?* *We called him Tortoise // **because** he taught us.* *Humpty Dumpty was very angry, // **though** he said nothing.*
		■ **independent clause + dependent non-finite clause**	***Burning with curiosity**, she ran across the field after it.* *She walked sadly down the middle, **wondering how she was ever to get out again.*** *Then Alice dodged behind a great thistle, **to keep herself from being run over.***
		■ **Independent clause + non-defining relative clause**	*'We indeed!' cried the Mouse, **who was trembling down to the end of his tail.***
	Other ways of organising the structure a sentence	■ **Interrupting clause**	*She had never forgotten that, **if you drink much from a bottle marked 'poison,'** it is almost certain to disagree with you.* *Both footmen, **Alice noticed**, had powdered hair that curled all over their heads.*
'How can we quote or report what someone says or thinks?'	**projecting**		
	– quoting (direct speech)	**quoted clause + quoting clause**	*'Stuff and nonsense!' // said Alice loudly.* *'A dear little crab!' // thought Alice.*
	– reporting (indirect speech)	**reporting clause + reported clause**	*Alice said // that there was no use trying.* *Alice wondered // how he could keep his balance.*

3 LANGUAGE FOR INTERACTING WITH OTHERS

Interpersonal language resources are used to interact in various ways with others depending on the tenor of the situation.

FUNCTION	REALISED TYPICALLY BY THE GRAMMATICAL CLASS OF :	EXAMPLE
Patterns of interaction		
providing information **(statement)**	clause (declarative)	*He went to bed early that night.*
requesting information **(question)**	clause (interrogative)	*Are you going to bed?*
asking someone to do something **(command)**	clause (imperative)	*Go to bed!*
offering to do something **(offer)**	various clause types	*Do you want a drink of water?*
indirect speech functions	various clause types	*Could you turn off the light? (question as command)*
'I'/'You' relationships	speech role pronouns	*Can I get **you** something?*
terms of address	vocatives	***Mum**, can you get the phone? Okay, **Lazybones**.*
Expressing attitudes		
expressing emotions	various language resources	***I hate** snails. [verb] I'm **fond** of her. [adjective] Her **fear** was palpable. [noun] He spoke **wistfully**. [adverb]*
evaluating qualities	various language resources	*A **stylish** sofa [aesthetics]; a **well-designed** car [composition]; a **fascinating** theory [reaction]; a **significant** breakthrough [social value]*
judging behaviour	various language resources	*He writes **well** [capacity]; she is **very brave** [tenacity]; a **deserving** winner [social esteem]; a **liar** and a **cheat** [ethics]*
Adjusting the strength and focus		
boosting	eg intensifying adverbs; repetition; quantification; extent	***incredibly** interesting; a **mad, mad** world; **thousands** of fans; for **miles and miles***
softening	eg downtoning adverbs; repetition; quantification; extent	***slightly** interesting; a **teeny weeny** bit; **only a couple of** fans; that's **only half** the story*
focusing	eg focusing adverbs / adjectives	***exactly** right; a **true** friend*
blurring	eg blurring adverbs / adjectives	*I **kind** of like him; it's **sort** of pathetic*

Engaging with other perspectives

asserting	bare assertion	It's true.
attributing	eg reporting verbs; adverbials of angle; nominalised sayings & thoughts	*He said* that it's true. *He thinks* it's true. *According to him*, it's true. *His claim* is that it is true.
establishing the tone	eg comment adverbials	*Surprisingly* it's true. It's true *unfortunately*.
allowing for other possibilities; indicating degree of certainty	modality evidentiality	It *might* be true. It's *probably* true. *Surely* it's true. It *must* be true. It's *seems* to be true. *Apparently* it's true.
making negative utterances	polarity – positive and negative	It's *not* true.

4 LANGUAGE FOR CREATING COHESIVE AND COHERENT TEXTS

Textual language resources are used to develop coherent texts in a variety of modes and media.

PROBE QUESTION	FUNCTION	TYPICALLY EXPRESSED BY:	EXAMPLE
Information flow			
'How can we manage the flow of information through the text?'	to indicate the 'point of departure' of a text ('text opener')	eg: a 'foreshadowing' move in the introduction indicating how the text will unfold.	See analysed text (Chapter 5 p.149)
	to indicate the 'point of departure' of a paragraph ('paragraph opener')	eg a move in the paragraph linking back to the overall theme and predicting the development of the paragraph ('topic sentence')	
	to indicate the 'point of departure' of a sentence ('sentence opener')	eg the beginning of the sentence ('Theme')	
Cohesion			
'How can we make links between items within a text?'	to refer back to something already mentioned	various cohesive devices (eg pronouns, determiners, comparatives)	See analysed text on p. 192
	to make links by omitting or substituting words	ellipsis and substitution	
	to connect stretches of text	text connectives	
	to create patterns of vocabulary items in a text	repetition collocation (predictable associations) synonyms antonyms part-whole relations class-subclass relations	

Epilogue: The language of literary texts

Given the prominence of literature in the English curriculum, it was felt that the analysis of a literary text would provide a useful focus for illustrating how all the different functions of language work together in the production of texts that vividly represent experience, that are interpersonally rich, and that are coherently crafted.

The various analyses of the text (adapted from *The Image of the Lost Soul* by Saki http://www.short-stories.co.uk) serve to provide the reader with further examples of the grammatical features covered in this book.

Achieving social purposes

A major social purpose of story genres is to entertain. They do so primarily by reflecting on the kinds of complications that arise in our lives and how they are resolved in various ways. In analysing any genre, we look at the stages it goes through in achieving its purpose. In the case of *The Image of the Lost Soul*, the staging of the story is relatively simple, with an Orientation introducing the physical setting (the cathedral with its parapets and statues) and the main characters (the Lost Soul and the little bird).

The Complication builds up slowly through a number of phases. The loving friendship between the statue and the bird appears too good to last – and the mutterings of the pigeons and the warning of the cathedral bell give a premonition of impending tragedy. This culminates in the imprisonment of the little bird, signalled by 'one chilly day'. The Complication is not, in fact, a single event, but is the outcome of a doomed alliance.

The Resolution of the problem – an inappropriate relationship – is the inevitable parting and death of the little bird and its protector.

The Image Of The Lost Soul by Saki

Orientation (introduces main character/s; setting)	There were a number of carved stone figures placed at intervals along the parapets of the old cathedral. Some of them represented angels, others represented kings and bishops, and nearly all looked pious or exalted. But one figure low down on the cold north side of the building had neither wings, nor crown, nor mitre, and its face was hard and bitter and downcast. It must be a demon, cooed the fat blue pigeons that sunned themselves all day on the ledges of the parapet. But the old belfry jackdaw, who was an authority on religious architecture, declared it was a lost soul. And that was the end of the matter.
	One autumn day there fluttered onto the cathedral roof a tiny, sweet-voiced bird that had wandered away from the bare fields in search of a winter roosting-place. It tried to rest its tired body under the shade of a great angel-wing or to nestle in the sculptured folds of a kingly robe, but the fat pigeons hustled it away from wherever it settled. No respectable bird sang with so much feeling, they cheeped one to another, and the wanderer had to move on.
	Only the figure of the Lost Soul offered a place of refuge. The pigeons did not consider that it was safe to perch on a statue that leaned so far out from the

cathedral, and was, besides, too much in the shadow. Its arms were folded as if in defiance and their angle made a snug resting-place for the little bird. Every evening it crept trustfully into its corner against the stone breast of the image, and the troubled eyes seemed to keep watch over its slumbers. The lonely bird grew to love its lonely protector, and during the day it would sit from time to time on the statue's head or shoulder and trill forth its sweetest music in grateful thanks for its nightly shelter. And the wild troubled face gradually seemed to lose some of its hardness and unhappiness. At evening, when the vesper-bell was ringing and the great grey bats slid out of their hiding-places in the belfry roof, the brighteyed bird would return, twitter a few sleepy notes, and nestle into the arms that were waiting for him. Those were happy days for the Dark Image. Only the great bell of the Cathedral rang out daily its mocking message, "After joy ... sorrow."

Complication (the little bird is captured)

One chilly day, the folk in the verger's lodge noticed a little brown bird flitting about the Cathedral, and admired its beautiful singing. "But it is a pity," they lamented, "that all that birdsong should be lost and wasted far out of hearing." So they captured the bird and put it in a little wire cage outside the lodge door.

That night the little songster was missing from its usual resting place, and the Dark Image knew more than ever the bitterness of loneliness. Perhaps his little friend had been killed by a prowling cat or hurt by a stone. Perhaps ... perhaps he had flown elsewhere, he mused forlornly. But when morning came, a faint heart-aching message from the prisoner in the wire cage far below floated up to him. And every day, at high noon, when the sparrows were washing themselves in the street-puddles, the song of the little bird came up to the heights of the cathedral – a song of hunger and longing and hopelessness, a cry that could never be answered. The pigeons remarked, between mealtimes, that the statue was leaning forward more than ever.

Resolution (bird dies of loneliness and statue crumbles – but the pigeons continue as before)

One day no song came up from the little wire cage. It was the coldest day of the winter, and the pigeons and sparrows on the Cathedral roof looked anxiously on all sides for scraps of food.

"Have the lodge-folk thrown out anything on to the dust-heap?" inquired one pigeon of another which was peering over the edge of the parapet.

"Only a little dead bird," was the answer.

There was a crackling sound in the night on the cathedral roof. The belfry jackdaw said the frost was affecting the stonework. In the morning the birds saw that the Figure of the Lost Soul had toppled from its cornice and lay now in a broken mass on the dust-heap outside the verger's lodge.

"It is just as well," cooed the fat pigeons, after they had peered at the shattered remains for some minutes; "now we shall have a nice angel up there. Certainly they will put an angel there."

"After joy ... sorrow," rang out the great bell.

Representing experience: Creating story worlds

Here the text has been analysed to show the main resources for building up a story world: 'What's happening?' (the Processes); 'Who/what is involved?' (the Participants); and 'What are the surrounding details?' (the Circumstances). The analysis is provided for the benefit of those who are interested in further examples of clauses and how they represent experience. It is not necessarily recommended that students be asked to undertake such detailed analyses of whole texts (unless they might find it useful or interesting). In the left-hand column, the type of process that the clause represents is indicated.[1]

Note: the following typographical conventions have been used in this analysis.

Processes (verb groups)

Participants (noun groups and <u>adjective groups</u>)

<u>Circumstances (adverbs/adverb groups, noun groups, and prepositional phrases</u> – note that prepositional phrases consist of a preposition + a noun group – these noun groups haven't been analysed)

[[embedded clauses]] – these haven't been analysed in further detail

[embedded phrase in a noun group][2]

« interrupting clause »

// – separates two clauses

Conjunctions (and 'there' as in 'there is' / 'there are') not analysed

Some interpersonal features (eg 'perhaps') – not analysed

'existing' clause	There *were* **a number of carved stone figures [[placed at intervals along the parapets of the old cathedral]]**.
relating clause	**Some of them** *represented* **angels,**
relating clause	**others** *represented* **kings and bishops,**
relating clause	and **nearly all** *looked* <u>**pious or exalted**</u>.
relating clause *(possessive)*	But **one figure low down on the cold north side of the building** *had* **neither wings, nor crown, nor mitre,**
relating clause	and **its face** *was* <u>**hard and bitter and downcast**</u>.
relating clause	**It** *must be* **a demon,**
saying clause	*cooed* **the fat blue pigeons [[that sunned themselves all day on the ledges of the parapet]]**.
saying clause «*relating clause*»	But **the old belfry jackdaw, «who** *was* **an authority [on religious architecture]»,** *declared*
relating clause	**it** *was* **a lost soul.**
relating clause	And **that** *was* **the end [of the matter]**.
action clause	<u>One autumn day</u> there *fluttered* <u>onto the cathedral roof</u> **a tiny, sweet-voiced bird [[that had wandered away from the bare fields in search of a winter roosting-place]]**.

---

[1] The term 'process' is often used to refer to a whole clause rather than simply the verb group.
[2] Not all these have been analysed to avoid over-cluttering.

action clause	**It** *tried to rest* **its tired body** <u>under the shade [of a great angel-wing]</u>
action clause	or *to nestle* in the sculptured folds [of a kingly robe],
action clause	but **the fat pigeons** *hustled* **it** <u>away from [[wherever it settled]].</u>
action clause	**No respectable bird** *sang* <u>with so much feeling,</u>
saying clause	**they** *cheeped* **one to another**.
action clause	And **the wanderer** *had to move on*.
action clause	**Only the figure [of the Lost Soul]** *offered* **a place [of refuge]**.
sensing clause	**The pigeons** *did not consider*
relating clause	that it was <u>safe</u> [[to perch on a statue [[that leaned so far out from the cathedral // and was, besides, too much in the shadow]]]].
action clause	**Its arms** *were folded* <u>as if in defiance</u>
relating clause	and **their angle** *made* **a snug resting-place [for the little bird]**.
action clause	<u>Every evening</u> **it** *crept* <u>trustfully into its corner [against the stone breast of the image],</u>
action clause	and **the troubled eyes** *seemed to keep watch* <u>over its slumbers</u>.
sensing clause	**The lonely bird** *grew to love* **its lonely protector**,
action clause	and <u>during the day</u> **it** *would sit* <u>from time to time on the statue's head or shoulder</u>
action clause	and *trill forth* **its sweetest music** <u>in grateful thanks for its nightly shelter</u>.
action clause	And **the wild troubled face** <u>gradually</u> *seemed to lose* **some of its hardness and unhappiness**.
action clause	<u>At evening</u>, when **the vesper-bell** *was ringing*
action clause	and **the great grey bats** *slid* <u>out of their hiding-places [in the belfry roof],</u>
action clause	**the brighteyed bird** *would return*,
action clause	*twitter* **a few sleepy notes**,
action clause	and *nestle* <u>into the arms [[that were waiting for him]].</u>
relating clause	**Those** *were* **happy days for the Dark Image**.
saying clause	**Only the great bell [of the Cathedral]** *rang out* <u>daily</u> **its mocking message**, "After joy ... sorrow."
sensing clause	<u>One chilly day</u>, **the folk in the verger's lodge** *noticed* **a little brown bird [[flitting about the Cathedral]]**,
sensing clause	and *admired* **its beautiful singing**.
relating clause	"But **it** *is* **a pity**," «they *lamented*», "[[that all that birdsong should be lost and wasted far out of hearing.]]"
«saying clause»	
action clause	So **they** *captured* **the bird**
action clause	and *put* **it** <u>in a little wire cage outside the lodge door</u>.
relating clause	<u>That night</u> **the little songster** *was* <u>missing [from its usual resting place],</u>
sensing clause	and **the Dark Image** *knew* <u>more than ever</u> **the bitterness [of loneliness]**.
action clause	Perhaps **his little friend** *had been killed* **by a prowling cat**
action clause	or *hurt* **by a stone**.
action clause	Perhaps ... perhaps **he** *had flown* <u>elsewhere,</u>
sensing clause	**he** *mused* forlornly.
action clause	But «when **morning** *came*,» **a faint heart-aching message [from the prisoner**
«action clause»	**[in the wire cage far below]]** *floated* <u>up to him</u>.
action clause	And <u>every day, at high noon</u>, «when **the sparrows** *were washing* **themselves**
«action clause»	in the street-puddles,» **the song [of the little bird]** *came up* <u>to the heights</u>

	[of the cathedral] – **a song [of hunger and longing and hopelessness], a cry [[that could never be answered]]**.
saying clause	**The pigeons** remarked, between mealtimes,
action clause	that **the statue** was leaning forward more than ever.
action clause	One day **no song** came up from the little wire cage.
relating clause	**It** was **the coldest day [of the winter]**,
action clause	and **the pigeons and sparrows [on the Cathedral roof]** looked anxiously on all sides for scraps of food.
action clause	"Have **the lodge-folk** thrown out **anything** on to the dust-heap?"
saying clause	inquired **one pigeon** of another [[which was peering over the edge of the parapet]].
relating clause	"**Only a little dead bird**," was **the answer.**
'existing' clause	There was **a crackling sound** in the night on the cathedral roof.
saying clause	**The belfry jackdaw** said
action clause	**the frost** was affecting **the stonework.**
sensing clause	In the morning **the birds** saw
action clause	that **the Figure of the Lost Soul** had toppled from its cornice
action clause	and lay now in a broken mass on the dust-heap [outside the verger's lodge].
relating clause	"**It** is just as well,"
saying clause	cooed **the fat pigeons,**
action clause	after **they** had peered at the shattered remains for some minutes;
relating clause	"now **we** shall have **a nice angel** up there.
action clause	Certainly **they** will put **an angel** there."
minor clause	"After joy . . . sorrow,"
saying clause	rang out **the great bell.**

Processes

In the Orientation, the clauses are mainly 'relating' ones, whose function is to build up a description of the characters and setting. Note that the descriptive details are not selected randomly – they provide a context for interpreting the theme of the text.

Once the activity gets underway, we find a number of 'action' clauses, with well-chosen action verbs/verb groups. The tiny bird *fluttered* onto the cathedral roof and *tried to rest* its tired body, but the pigeons *hustled* it away so it had to *move on*. The Lost Soul *offered* a place of refuge and *seemed to keep watch over* its slumbers while the bird would *trill forth* its song, *twitter* a few notes, and *nestle* into the waiting arms of the statue. (Note that processes such as 'sing', 'twitter' and 'trill forth' can be seen as 'behavioural verbs'.)

Throughout the story, various participants reflect on and evaluate what is happening, using saying processes (the pigeons *cooed* and *cheeped* and *remarked* and *inquired*, the jackdaw *declared* and *said*) as well as sensing processes (the pigeons *did not consider*, the lodge folk *noticed*, *admired* and *lamented*, and the statue *knew* and *mused*).

Circumstances

Circumstances of place track the changing location of the action. The little bird fluttered *onto the cathedral roof* and tried to find shelter *under the shade of a great angel-wing* and *in the sculptured folds of a kingly robe*) but is hustled *away from wherever it settled*. When the Lost Soul offered refuge, the bird would creep *into its corner against the stone breast of the image* and would nestle *into the arms that were waiting for him*. This haven is disrupted, however, when the bird is captured and placed *in a little wire cage outside the lodge door*, from where his song reached *up to the heights of the cathedral*. One day its song no longer came up *from the little wire cage* and the little bird was thrown *on to the dust-heap* and not long after, the shattered remains of the statue were also found *on the dust-heap outside the verger's lodge*.

Circumstances of time locate the activity of the little bird in terms of the regular daily routine that develops, when *during the day* it *would sit* and *trill forth* its music and *At evening would twitter* a few notes and then *nestle* into the statue's arms. This routine is interrupted, however, by another Circumstance of time – but in this case a specific, ominous time: *One chilly day*. The new routine of imprisonment now replaces the old routine – *every day*, *at high noon*, the bird's song would float up to the statue. But again, another Circumstance of time interrupts: *One day* the song stopped and *in the night* there was a crackling sound and *In the morning* the shattered remains of the statue were found outside the verger's lodge.

Participants

Even in such a short text, the author, Saki, manages to bring the characters to life through his choice of highly descriptive noun groups. The statue is characterised as **a demon** and **a lost soul**, with **troubled eyes** and a **wild troubled face**. The little bird is described as **a tiny, sweet-voiced bird, the brighteyed bird** and **the little songster**. Their relationship is developed when the statue offers **a place of refuge** and **a snug resting-place** for the bird to rest **its tired body**, becoming **its lonely protector, its nightly shelter**. When they were separated, the bird's anguish is captured in noun groups such as **a faint heart-aching message from the prisoner in the wire cage far below, a song of hunger and longing and hopelessness**, and **a cry that could never be answered**.

One area of literary language that we haven't touched on previously is the use of figurative language. This generally has the function of operating at different levels[3] – inviting the listener/reader to engage with more than one meaning at once, both in the creativity of everyday conversation and in literary texts. While literal language 'means what it says', figurative language 'doesn't mean what it says'. An understanding of figurative language depends largely on being able to 'read' the context – both at the level of the culture and the particular situation.

---

[3] Often referred to as 'tropes' – the use of language in other than its literal sense.

TROUBLESHOOTING

Students who are unfamiliar with the cultural references, the literary allusions and social values will have difficulty dealing with figurative language and will need explicit support.

> Identify how rhetorical devices are used to persuade and how different layers of meaning are developed through the use of metaphor, irony and parody [Year 8]

In relation to the story above, 'Saki' is the pseudonym of Hector Hugh Munro, who was writing short stories in the late 19th century. Munro was believed to be homosexual – at a time when sexual activity between men was a crime. If this is the case, then the story above can be read on different levels, perhaps as an allegorical statement about a doomed loving relationship between two outcasts rejected by the cold stone-like figures representing the authority of the church and the state, and both dying in pain on the dust-heap after the fleeting joy.

Here, then, experience is being represented as 'multi-layered' and we have to read the text on more than one level. As an allegory, we would notice the metaphors of winter as a time of death, of the cage as a prison, of the bell as a harbinger of tragedy. We would see the irony in the pigeons hoping for an angel statue as a replacement – when the Lost Soul was, in fact, such a figure. We would be prompted to ask questions about the 'hidden' meanings:

> *Who do the pigeons represent?*
>
> *Who is the pompous jackdaw, parodied as 'an authority on religious architecture'?*
>
> *What were the 'bare fields' that the little bird was escaping from?*
>
> *Does the fact that the statue 'leaned so far out from the cathedral' suggest that it was inclining away from the teachings of the church?*
>
> *Why could the imprisoned bird's cry 'never be answered'?*

Connecting clauses

The ways in which clauses are combined in this story is, on the whole, quite straightforward. Many, in fact, are single clauses (simple sentences) – often used for dramatic effect:

> And that was the end of the matter.

Other clauses are combined into compound sentences using coordinating conjunctions (eg *and, but, so, or*) similar to the way we combine clauses in spoken language:

> It tried to rest its tired body under the shade of a great angel-wing
>
> **or** to nestle in the sculptured folds of a kingly robe,
>
> **but** the fat pigeons hustled it away from wherever it settled.

There are only a couple of instances of complex sentences, combining an independent clause with a dependent clause – and the dependent clauses are both 'when' clauses of time, which are typical of storytelling:

> But when morning came, a faint heart-aching message from the prisoner in the wire cage far below floated up to him.
>
> And every day, at high noon, when the sparrows were washing themselves in the street-puddles, the song of the little bird came up to the heights of the cathedral – a song of hunger and longing and hopelessness, a cry that could never be answered.

There is one instance of a compound-complex sentence, where an independent clause is related to at least one other independent clause and at least one other dependent clause. The following clause has three independent clauses and two dependent clauses:

> At evening, when the vesper-bell was ringing *(dependent)*
>
> and (when) the great grey bats slid out of their hiding-places in the belfry roof, *(dependent)*
>
> the brighteyed bird would return, *(independent)*
>
> (and) twitter a few sleepy notes, *(independent)*
>
> and nestle into the arms that were waiting for him. *(independent)*

Clauses are also related to each other in terms of direct speech (quoting clauses and quoted clauses) and indirect speech (reporting clauses and reported clauses) – another typical feature of stories:

> The pigeons remarked *(reporting clause)*
>
> that the statue was leaning forward more than ever. *('what was reported')*

There are several examples of embedded clauses, including those that are part of the noun group:

> There were a number of **carved stone figures [[placed at intervals along the parapets of the old cathedral]]**.

In another case, there are quite complex embeddings, with a couple of embedded clauses within another embedded clause:

> The pigeons did not consider that it was **safe [[to perch on a statue [[that leaned so far out from the cathedral // and was, besides, too much in the shadow]]]]**.

Here, [[to perch on a statue ...]] is elaborating on the adjective 'safe'. The pair of clauses – [[that leaned so far out from the cathedral // and (that) was, besides too much in the shadow]] are part of the noun group, telling more about the statue.

There are also embedded clauses that take on the role of Participant[4] (answering the probe question 'What?'), eg:

> "But it is a pity **[[that all that birdsong should be lost and wasted far out of hearing]]**."

---

[4] These are sometimes referred to as 'fact clauses' or 'noun clauses'.

In this case, 'it' is acting as a placeholder[5] and the sentence could have been rewritten in the following manner, answering the question '**What** is a pity?':

But	[[that all that birdsong should be lost and wasted far out of hearing]]	*is*	**a pity.**
	Participant	Process (relating)	Participant

These are not the kind of grammatical analyses we would expect students to be concerned with. They are included here because such complex structures are found in authentic texts and teachers need to be aware that, even in what appears to be a grammatically simple story, there are certain structures that might prove difficult for some students to read.

Another potential source of reading difficulties is clauses that interrupt another clause. There are a few cases of interrupting clauses (and phrases) in this story that disrupt fluency when reading:

> But the old belfry jackdaw, «who was an authority on religious architecture», declared ...

Here the independent clause – But the old belfry jackdaw declared – has been interrupted by a dependent clause[6] (who was an authority on religious architecture).

Overall, we could say that the clauses in this story generally form either simple sentences or compound sentences. This is fairly typical of short stories, where there is not a great deal of complexity in the logical relationship between clauses (compared to, for example, an argument or explanation). There are, however, a number of quite complex sentence structures that teachers would need to be aware of, which are demonstrated in the table that follows.

simple sentence	There *were* **a number of carved stone figures [[placed at intervals along the parapets of the old cathedral]]**.
compound sentence	**Some of them** *represented* **angels,** **others** *represented* **kings and bishops,** **and nearly all** *looked* <u>**pious or exalted**</u>.
compound sentence	But **one figure low down on the cold north side of the building** *had* **neither wings, nor crown, nor mitre,** **and its face** *was* <u>**hard and bitter and downcast**</u>.
reported clause	**It** *must be* **a demon,**
reporting clause	*cooed* **the fat blue pigeons [[that sunned themselves all day on the ledges of the parapet]]**.
reporting clause «*interrupting clause*»	But **the old belfry jackdaw,** «**who** *was* **an authority [on religious architecture]**», *declared*
reported clause	**it** *was* **a lost soul.**
simple sentence	And **that** *was* **the end of the matter.**

---

[5]   Sometimes called 'dummy it'.
[6]   In this case, a non-defining relative clause.

simple sentence	One autumn day there *fluttered* onto the cathedral roof **a tiny, sweet-voiced bird** [[that had wandered away from the bare fields in search of a winter roosting-place]].
compound sentence	**It** *tried to rest* **its tired body** under the shade of a great angel-wing or *to nestle* in the sculptured folds of a kingly robe, but **the fat pigeons** *hustled* it away from [[wherever it settled]].
reported clause	**No respectable bird** *sang* with so much feeling,
reporting clause	**they** *cheeped* one to another.
simple sentence	And **the wanderer** *had to move on.*
simple sentence	**Only the figure** [of the Lost Soul] *offered* **a place** [of refuge].
reporting clause	**The pigeons** *did not consider*
reported clause	that **it** *was* **safe** [[to perch on a statue [[that leaned so far out from the cathedral]] // and was, besides, too much in the shadow]].
compound sentence	**Its arms** *were folded* as if in defiance and **their angle** *made* **a snug resting-place** [for the little bird].
compound sentence	Every evening **it** *crept* trustfully into its corner [against the stone breast of the image], and **the troubled eyes** *seemed to keep watch over* its slumbers.
compound sentence	**The lonely bird** *grew to love* **its lonely protector**, and during the day **it** *would sit* from time to time on the statue's head or shoulder and *trill forth* **its sweetest music** in grateful thanks for its nightly shelter.
simple sentence	And **the wild troubled face** gradually *seemed to lose* **some of its hardness and unhappiness.**
compound-complex sentence (with interrupting clauses)	At evening, «when **the vesper-bell** *was ringing* // and **the great grey bats** *slid* out of their hiding-places in the belfry roof,» **the brighteyed bird** *would return, twitter* **a few sleepy notes**, and *nestle* into the arms [[that were waiting for him]].
simple sentence	**Those** *were* **happy days for the Dark Image.**
simple sentence	**Only the great bell of the Cathedral** *rang out* daily **its mocking message,** "After joy . . . sorrow."
compound sentence	One chilly day, **the folk in the verger's lodge** *noticed* **a little brown bird** [[flitting about the Cathedral]], and *admired* **its beautiful singing.**
reported clause *«interrupting reporting clause»*	"But **it** *is* **a pity**," «they *lamented*», "[[that all that birdsong should be lost and wasted far out of hearing.]]"
compound sentence	So **they** *captured* **the bird** and *put* it in a little wire cage outside the lodge door.
compound sentence	That night **the little songster** *was missing* from its usual resting place, and **the Dark Image** *knew* more than ever **the bitterness of loneliness.**
compound sentence	Perhaps **his little friend** *had been killed* **by a prowling cat** or *hurt* **by a stone.**

> its **sweetest** music
>
> the **coldest** day of the winter

The strength can also be boosted through rhetorical patterns such as 'the rule of three':

> neither wings, nor crown, nor mitre
>
> its face was hard and bitter and downcast
>
> a song of hunger and longing and hopelessness

Lowering the strength

The significance of the bird is dismissed as '**Only** a little dead bird' – in this case, not so much a focusing resource (as above) as a 'diminisher'.

Opening up and contracting the interaction

Opening up the interaction: Modality and evidentiality[8]

Occasionally low modality is used to open up the space for other possibilities. With the arrival of the little bird, the statue's face <u>seemed</u> to lose some of its hardness and unhappiness. And when the little bird disappears, the statue ponders the possibilities:

> <u>Perhaps</u> his little friend had been killed by a prowling cat
>
> or hurt by a stone.
>
> <u>Perhaps</u> ... <u>perhaps</u> he had flown elsewhere.

Closing down the interaction: Negatives

The negative has been used to open up the possibility of an alternative but then to close it down. When the statue is described, for example, as having neither wings, nor crown, nor mitre, the alternative is implied that angels have wings, kings have crowns and bishops have mitres, but the Lost Soul had none of these. In contrast to the times when the little bird sang every day, *One day no song came up from the little wire cage.*

Creating cohesive texts: Developing texture

The following analysis identifies the various devices drawn on to make the text cohesive in the way we would expect of the written mode[9].

Note: the following typographical conventions have been used in this analysis.

> Ellipsed items have been indicated by 're-inserting' them in blue and ~~struck-through~~.
>
> Reference items (eg pronouns) are in *italics*.
>
> The items being referred to are <u>underlined</u>.
>
> Text connectives are in **bold**.

---

[8] Evidentiality refers to the use of words such as 'seem', 'appear', 'suggests', and 'apparently'.
[9] Technically, cohesion occurs between sentences. Here, however, the analysis includes cohesive ties within sentences in order to illustrate more examples of cohesive devices.

There were a number of carved stone figures placed at intervals along the parapets of the old cathedral. *Some of them* represented angels, *others* represented kings and bishops, and *nearly all* of the figures looked pious or exalted. **But** one figure low down on the cold north side of the building had neither wings, nor crown, nor mitre, and *its* face was hard and bitter and downcast. *It* must be a demon, cooed the fat blue pigeons that sunned themselves all day on the ledges of the parapet. **But** the old belfry jackdaw, who was an authority on religious architecture, declared *it* was a lost soul. **And** *that* was the end of the matter.

One autumn day there fluttered onto the cathedral roof a tiny, sweet-voiced bird that had wandered away from the bare fields in search of a winter roosting-place. *It* tried to rest *its* tired body under the shade of a great angel-wing or it tried to nestle in the sculptured folds of a kingly robe, but the fat pigeons hustled *it* away from wherever *it* settled. No respectable bird sang with so much feeling, *they* cheeped one to another, and the wanderer had to move on.

Only the figure of the Lost Soul offered a place of refuge. The pigeons did not consider that it was safe to perch on a statue that leaned so far out from the cathedral, and which was, besides, too much in the shadow. *Its* arms were folded as if in defiance and *their* angle made a snug resting-place for the little bird. Every evening *it* crept trustfully into *its* corner against the stone breast of the image, and the troubled eyes seemed to keep watch over *its* slumbers. The lonely bird grew to love *its* lonely protector, and during the day *it* would sit from time to time on the statue's head or shoulder and trill forth *its* sweetest music in grateful thanks for *its* nightly shelter. **And** the wild troubled face gradually seemed to lose some of *its* hardness and unhappiness. At evening, when the vesper-bell was ringing and the great grey bats slid out of *their* hiding-places in the belfry roof, the brighteyed bird would return, twitter a few sleepy notes, and nestle into the arms that were waiting for *him*. *Those* were happy days for the Dark Image. Only the great bell of the Cathedral rang out daily *its* mocking message, "After joy … sorrow."

One chilly day, the folk in the verger's lodge noticed a little brown bird flitting about the Cathedral, and they admired *its* beautiful singing. "But it is a pity," *they* lamented, "that all *that* birdsong should be lost and wasted far out of hearing." **So** *they* captured the bird and they put *it* in a little wire cage outside the lodge door.

That night the little songster was missing from *its* usual resting place, and the Dark Image knew more than ever the bitterness of loneliness. Perhaps *his* little friend had been killed by a prowling cat or hurt by a stone. Perhaps . . . perhaps *he* had flown elsewhere, *he* mused forlornly. **But** when morning came, a faint heart-aching message from the prisoner in the wire cage far below floated up to *him*. **And** every day, at high noon, when the sparrows were washing themselves in the street-puddles, the song of the little bird came up to the heights of the cathedral – a song of hunger and longing and hopelessness, a cry that could never be answered. The pigeons remarked, between mealtimes, that the statue was leaning forward more than ever.

One day no song came up from the little wire cage. *It* was the coldest day of the winter, and the pigeons and sparrows on the Cathedral roof looked anxiously on all sides for scraps of food.

"Have the lodge-folk thrown out anything on to the dust-heap?" inquired one pigeon of another which was peering over the edge of the parapet.

They have thrown "Only a little dead bird," was the answer.

There was a crackling sound in the night on the cathedral roof. The belfry jackdaw said the frost was affecting the stonework. In the morning the birds saw that the Figure of the Lost Soul had toppled from *its* cornice and lay now in a broken mass on the dust-heap outside the verger's lodge.

"*It* is just as well," cooed the fat pigeons, after *they* had peered at the shattered remains for some minutes; "now *we* shall have a nice angel up *there*. Certainly *they* will put an angel there."

"After joy ... sorrow," rang out the great bell.

Reference

Given the brevity of the story, there is not a great deal of cohesion created through reference items such as pronouns, demonstratives and possessives. The arrows in the text above show the various reference links being made between items.

Ellipsis

There are very few instances of ellipsis ('leaving words out', forcing the reader to retrieve the meaning from the surrounding text).

Text connectives

Text connectives are restricted to coordinating conjunctions (*and, but* and *so*), giving a 'spoken' flavour to the text.

Word patterns

The main cohesive device used in this text is the creation of patterns through various kinds of relationships between vocabulary items.

Things that are similar ('synonyms')

By referring to something using different terms, we create a cohesive tie. The Lost Soul, for example, is referred to as:

> The Lost Soul
>
> one figure
>
> a demon
>
> a lost soul
>
> the figure of the Lost Soul
>
> a statue that leaned so far out from the cathedral
>
> its lonely protector
>
> the Dark Image
>
> Figure of the Lost Soul

Similarly, the little bird is referred to by a variety of synonyms (or 'near-synonyms'):

> a tiny, sweet-voiced bird
>
> the wanderer
>
> the little bird
>
> The lonely bird
>
> the brighteyed bird
>
> a little brown bird
>
> the bird
>
> his little friend

the prisoner

a little dead bird

For some students – especially ESL learners – it is difficult to recognise that, for example, the 'wanderer' is the same as the 'his little friend' and the 'prisoner'.

Things that are opposite ('antonyms')

Cohesive links can also be created by making contrasts. 'Angels', for example, are an antonym of 'demon'. The 'snug resting place' is the opposite of 'a little wire cage'. And 'happiness' is opposed to 'the bitterness of loneliness'.

While not strictly antonyms, the lengthy noun group '**a number of carved stone figures placed at intervals along the parapets of the old cathedral**', which locates the angels, kings and bishops high on the parapets, contrasts with the noun group introducing the Lost Soul – **one figure low down on the cold north side of the building** – who is located in a lowly, dark and cold position. The adjective group describing the lofty statues – **pious or exalted –** reinforces the contrast with the Lost Soul, described as **hard and bitter and downcast**.

Similarly, the noun group describing the self-satisfied, well-fed pigeons – **the fat blue pigeons that sunned themselves all day on the ledges of the parapet** – contrasts with the tired, hungry wanderer – **a tiny, sweet-voiced bird that had wandered away from the bare fields in search of a winter roosting-place**.

Part-whole patterns

There are a few patterns in the text that relate things in terms of the whole and its parts:

the old cathedral

the parapets

the cold north side of the building

the ledges of the parapet

the vesper-bell

the belfry roof

the great bell of the Cathedral

the verger's lodge

the lodge door

the Cathedral roof

the edge of the parapet

its cornice

> **one figure**
>
> its face
>
> Its arms
>
> the stone breast of the image
>
> the troubled eyes
>
> the statue's head or shoulder
>
> the wild troubled face

Class-subclass patterns

Stories don't often have a dominant pattern of hierarchies. Here we find a couple of minor taxonomies such as the different types of birds:

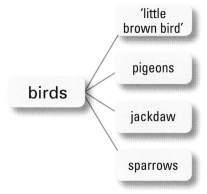

Repetition

There are words that are repeated in the text that give it a sense of unity. In literary texts, repetition is sometimes used for stylistic reasons, such as the repetition of the refrain 'After joy ... sorrow'.

References

Adams, C.V.A. (1958) *Nature is my Hobby,* Exeter, UK: A. Wheaton Publishers.

Atherton, G.F.A. (1919) *The Avalanche – A Mystery Story*, Accessed from Project Gutenberg http://www.gutenberg.org/catalog/world/readfile?fk_files = 1468576

Byrne, J.P. & Overton, W.F. (1988) 'Reasoning About Logical Connectives: A Developmental Analysis', *Journal of Experimental Child Psychology*, Volume 46, Issue 2, October 1988, Pages 194–218.

Burke, C. 'Newtown – A Fantasy' in *Wildlife in Newtown*, Newtown: Feakle Press

Chekhov, A. *A Day in the Country*, Accessed from Classic Literature, http://classiclit.about.com/library/bl-etexts/achekhov/bl-achek-daycountry.htm

Clark, E. (1971) 'On the Acquisition of the Meaning of *Before* and *After*', *Journal of Verbal Learning and Verbal Behavior*, Volume 10, Issue 3, June 1971, Pages 266–275.

Condon, W. (1990) *That Smell is My Brother,* Marrickville: Harcourt Brace Jovanovich.

Dahl, R. (1986) *Going Solo*, London: Puffin Books.

Dahl, R. (1991) 'Beware of the Dog', in *The Collected Short Stories of Roald Dahl*, USA: Penguin Books USA.

Davidson, A. (1984) *Understanding Mathematics 5: How Many*, Auckland: Shorthand Publications.

Derewianka, B. (1991) *Exploring How Texts Work*, Sydney: PETA.

Emerson, H. (1979) 'Children's Comprehension of 'Because' in Reversible and Non-reversible Sentences', *Journal of Child Language* (1979), 6: 279–300.

Fatcher, M (1989) 'The Skateboard' in *A Pocketful of Rhymes*, South Australia: Omnibus/Puffin.

Gallico, P. (1991) *Glorious Cats,* London: Aurum Press Ltd.

Grahame, K. (1983; 1908) *The Wind in the Willows* (abridged by Barbara Sleigh), Kent, UK: Hodder & Stoughton.

Halliday, M.A.K. & Matthiessen, C.M.I.M. (2004) *Introduction to Functional Grammar*, (3rd Edition), London: Arnold.

Hart-Smith, W. (2010) 'The Beach' in *The ABC Book of Australian Poetry*, compiled by Libby Hathorn, Sydney: HarperCollins.

Klein, R. (1988) *Boss of the Pool,* Ringwood: Penguin.

Kipling, R. (1894) 'Rikki-Tikki-Tavi' in *The Jungle Book* (Volume 2) Accessed from Project Gutenberg, http://www.gutenberg.org/files/236/236-h/236-h.htm

Lear, E. (1988; 1894) Edward Lear's *Nonsense Omnibus,* Leicester: Galley Press.

Martin, J.R. & White, P.R.R., 2005, *The Language of Evaluation, Appraisal in English*, Palgrave Macmillan, London & New York.

Milne, A.A. (1996; 1928) *The House at Pooh Corner,* Suffolk: Chancer Press.

Milne, A.A. (1926) *Winnie the Pooh,* Suffolk: Chancer Press.

Montgomery, L.M. *Anne of Green Gables* Accessed from Literature.org http://www.literature.org/authors/montgomery-lucy-maud/anne-of-green-gables/

Neimark, E.D. & Slotnick, N.S. (1970) 'Development of the Understanding of Logical Connectives', *Journal of Educational Psychology*, 61.

Norman, L. 'The Sea' in *My First Oxford Book of Poems*, compiled by John Foster, OUP.

Rowling, J.K. (1997) *Harry Potter and the Sorcerer's Stone*, London: Bloomsbury.

Sacco, K., Bucciarelli, M. & Adenzato, M. (2001) 'Mental Models and the Meaning of Connectives: A Study on Children, Adolescents and Adults', In: J.D. Moore and K. Stenning (eds.), 2001. *Proceedings of the Twenty-Third Conference of the Cognitive Science Society*. Mahwah, NJ, Lawrence Erlbaum Associates, 875–880.

Saxby, M. (ed) (1994) *My Country,* Melbourne: Macmillan.

Sternberg, R. (1979) 'Developmental Patterns in the Encoding and Combination of Logical Connectives' *Journal of Experimental Child Psychology* Volume 28, Issue 3, December 1979, Pages 469–498.

Talese, G. (2003) *The Gay Talese Reader: Portraits & Encounters,* Walker Publishing Company

Further reading

Butt, D., Fahey, R., Feez, S., Spinks, S. & Yallop, C. (2000) *Using Functional Grammar: An Explorer's Guide,* (2nd Edition), Sydney: National Centre for English Language Teaching and Research (NCELTR).

Christie, F. (2005) *Language Education in the Primary Years,* Sydney: University of NSW Press.

Coffin, C., Donohue, J., & North, S. (2009) *Exploring English Grammar: From Formal to Functional,* New York: Routledge.

Collerson, J. (1994) *English Grammar: A Functional Approach,* Sydney: PETA.

Collerson, J. (1997) *Grammar in Teaching,* Sydney: PETA.

Cusworth, R. (1994) What is a Functional Model of Language? *PEN 95,* Sydney: PETA.

Derewianka, B. (1991) *Exploring How Texts Work,* Sydney: PETA.

Schleppegrell, M. (2004) *The Language of Schooling: A Functional Linguistics Perspective,* NJ: Lawrence Erlbaum Associates.

Droga, L. & Humphrey, S. (2003) *Grammar and Meaning: An Introduction for Primary Teachers,* NSW: Target Texts.

Droga, L. & Humphrey, S. (2002) *Getting Started with Functional Grammar,* NSW: Target Texts.

Eggins, S. (2005) *An Introduction to Systemic Functional Linguistics,* (2nd Edition), London: Continuum.

Feez, S. (1998) *Text-based Syllabus Design.* Sydney: National Centre for English Language Teaching and Research (NCELTR).

Feez, S. (1998) *Writing Skills: Narrative and Non-Fiction Text Types,* Melbourne: Phoenix.

Halliday, M.A.K. & Matthiessen, C.M.I.M. (2004) *Introduction to Functional Grammar,* (3rd Edition), London: Arnold.

Humphrey, S., Love, K. & Droga, L. (2011) *Working Grammar: An Introduction for Secondary English Teachers,* Melbourne: Pearson.

Jones, R. & Lock, G. (2011) *Functional Grammar in the ESL Classroom: Noticing, Exploring and Practising,* UK: Palgrave Macmillan.

Martin, J.R. & Rose, D. (2007) *Working with Discourse: Meaning Beyond the Clause,* (2nd Edition), London: Continuum.

Martin, J.R. & Rose, D. (2008) *Genre Relations: Mapping Culture,* London: Equinox.

Martin, J.R. & White, P.R.R. (2005) *The Language of Evaluation: Appraisal in English,* UK & USA: Palgrave Macmillan.

Rossbridge, J. & Rushton, K. (2010) *Conversations about Text: Teaching Grammar Using Literary Texts,* Sydney: e:lit.

Thompson, G. (1996) *Introducing Functional Grammar,* London: Edward Arnold.

Unsworth, L. (Ed.) (1993) *Literacy Learning and Teaching: Language as Social Practice in the Primary School,* Melbourne: Macmillan.

Whittaker, R., O'Donnell, M. & McCabe, A. (2006) *Language and Literacy: Functional Approaches,* London: Continuum.

Index